C000005712

MISSING, BELIEVED WIPED

MISSING, BELIEVED WIPED

Searching for the Lost Treasures of British Television

Dick Fiddy

 Publishing

This book is dedicated to all my friends and colleagues at the BFI, and especially to my fellow traveller in the world of archive TV, Veronica Taylor, whose constant encouragement, help and friendship has proved invaluable.

IN MEMORY OF JOHN PLATT – ace researcher and all-round good guy

First published in 2001 by the
British Film Institute
21 Stephen Street, London W1T 1LN

The British Film Institute promotes greater understanding of,
and access to, film and moving image culture in the UK.

Copyright © Dick Fiddy 2001

Cover design: ketchup
Cover illustration: Peter Cook and Dudley Moore – *Not Only ... But Also* (BBC)

Set by ketchup, London
Printed in the UK by Cromwell Press, Trowbridge, Wiltshire.

British Library Cataloguing–in–Publication Data
A catalogue record for this book is available from the British Library
ISBN 0–85170–866–8 pbk
ISBN 0–85170–867–6 hbk

CONTENTS

PART ONE

THE STORY

INTRODUCTION

The early technical difficulties associated with the recording of live television programmes and the later injudicious wiping and junking policies of the major British broadcasters has meant that hundreds of thousands of hours of precious television material is missing from the official UK television archives. Nowadays such decisions to destroy vast stockpiles of programming are seen as scandalous, cultural vandalism on a grand scale, but, as explained later, there were mitigating circumstances – reasons that certainly seemed logical at the time. With hindsight it's easy to point the figure and badmouth the industry personnel responsible for such woeful destruction, but the story of this initiative is that of a treasure hunt rather than a witch hunt. It's of little use lamenting what went on, it's impossible to undo what has been done. A far better idea is try and reclaim as much of the missing material as possible. Hence, Missing, Believed Wiped.

The BFI's initiative was launched in 1993 (and was inspired by *Missing, Believed Lost*, an earlier BFI quest for some classic British movies), but the story of returning programmes goes back much further. By the early 1980s TV companies began to realise the folly of their earlier junking policies and started making efforts to track down some items they had wiped or destroyed. Their best hopes were with the foreign archives which may have held onto copies of programmes dumped by the UK broadcasters. These were by no mean co-ordinated efforts – more individual initiatives from various archive personnel. Such activity may have been prompted by the outrage of *Doctor Who* fans upon realising just how many episodes of their favourite series had been junked (nearly 150!), or perhaps by the news items that had been sparked by the revelation (by Peter Cook?) that much of his classic *Not Only … But Also* was missing from the archives. Certainly the burgeoning home video market may have also spurred some investigations as it became increasingly obvious that such archive programming could be worth considerable amounts of money.

So, the recovery of programmes was well underway before the Missing, Believed Wiped (MBW) initiative. The MBW launch meant that for the first time the search for missing programmes could be co-ordinated under one single umbrella. Broadcasting companies were somewhat limited in their ability to search out programmes many collectors or foreign archives which held lost material were reluctant to admit it to the copyright-owning broadcasters for fear of prosecution. Such fears may have been mostly unfounded but certain high-profile prosecutions in the collecting area did little to alleviate the tense atmosphere. By acting as a go-between, the BFI would find it easier to approach (and be approached) by those with something to hand back. The MBW initiative also came with a promise that any returned material would be copied and the original (or if preferable a best possible quality VHS copy) would be returned to the donor. The broadcasting companies would find it difficult to make such a promise as the properties in question were, of course, wholly owned by them. Although it was known that archivists would arrange (fairly unofficially) for some swap deals to be made on returned material (from private collectors), it was not an ideal relationship, whereas the BFI's involvement meant there was a better way of negotiating. This didn't mean that individual broadcasters ceased seeking out material, but it did mean that new avenues of contact were opened.

Missing, Believed Wiped launched to the press with a list of the 'top twenty' missing programmes (a list put together by the BFI's MBW team which attempted to cover various genres: comedy, drama, documentary, music, news etc.). This generated quite a lot of media interest and kick-started the initiative. By the time we organised the first MBW screening (at the National Film Theatre [NFT]) we had already been contacted by a number of individuals who, responding to the media coverage, thought they might be in possession of missing programmes. It was deemed essential to follow-up on the most intriguing items and to that end I was employed (under a part-time, six-month contract) to investigate further. This resulted in some significant recoveries (see the MBW event history). This initial follow-up period was important because we had so much response from the first wave of publicity. In subsequent years the flow had been more restrained allowing follow-up procedures to be carried out by National Film and Television Archive (NFTVA) staff as part of their normal work.

Then early 2001, just as this book was nearing completion, my colleagues at the BBC invited me, as a representative of the BFI, to a meeting to discuss their own version of Missing Believed Wiped, an initiative to be called 'Treasure Hunt'. Treasure Hunt (concerned with radio as well as TV) launched on 14 May 2001 in a wave of publicity and quickly led to the discovery of a few important missing programmes, precise details of which have come too late for inclusion in this book, although where possible the newly recovered material identified as 'missing' in these lists now bears a stamp reclassifying it as 'RECOVERED'

The purpose of this book is to highlight a clutch of the most precious missing material by giving details of these highly sought after programmes. It would be impossible of course to list everything that's AWOL, but by handpicking a few of the choicest morsels it's possible to give an idea of the depth and breadth of what has gone. More importantly, previous successes in relocating missing items suggest that some of these gems will have survived somewhere in some form and may be identified by the details given.

The message remains the same – if you think you are in possession of British television material missing from the official archives please contact:

Steve Bryant, Keeper of Television, 21 Stephen St., London W1T 1LN,
e-mail: steve.bryant@bfi.org.uk

or me, Dick Fiddy, National Film Theatre, London SE1 8XT
e-mail: dick.fiddy@bfi.org.uk

Dick Fiddy, London, August 2001

BACKGROUND

The First Era (1936–9)

In 1936 when the BBC began broadcasting (and the wording is critical here) *the world's first high definition, regular, public television service*, the medium was a very different beast to the one that beams multi-channels to today's living rooms. Initially, viewing was limited to two hours daily (3–4pm and 9–10pm) except Sundays (Sunday transmissions wouldn't begin until spring 1938). Controlled by radio broadcasters, and with wireless man Gerald Cock as the first director of the service, it was inevitable that television, in its infancy, would owe much to radio. Indeed television was referred to as 'wireless with pictures' and that was especially true when it came to light entertainment. Music Hall comedians like Tommy Handley (pre-*It's That Man Again*) and Gillie Potter ('reporting from Hogsnorton') had adapted their acts for radio and did likewise for the visual medium. The programme *Starlight* presented singers and cabaret artists, who were often using material they had used on the radio during the same week. Many radio programmes transferred to the small screen, albeit modestly in short segments, but the primitive scenery and bulky cameras meant that the ideas could never match visually the images that could be conjured up on the radio.

Although the notion of relying on proven talent and formats was appealing, it was the ideas specifically created for television that caused most impact. *Picture Page*, a magazine programme presenting visiting luminaries, was a notable success, and made a star out of its 'switchboard girl'

George Bernard Shaw and the cast of *How He Lied to Her Husband* – Greer Garson, Derek Williams, G. More O'Ferrall and D. A. Clarke-Smith.

Joan Miller who would link the items by making connections on a large switchboard. As the medium developed and the equipment became more mobile, so the programme-makers became more ambitious and in the course of those first three years over 300 full-length plays were transmitted including George Bernard Shaw's *How He Lied To Her Husband* (7/7/37 – which Shaw himself turned up to see and afterwards commented on the production on-screen); Reginald Tate in Sherrif's *Journey's End* (11/11/37); Karel Capek's science fiction play *R.U.R.*; Maugham's *The Breadwinner* (7/11/38) and the first full-length musical play seen on TV, the 175 minute *Magyar Melody* (27/3/39) broadcast from His Majesty's Theatre. Plus there was television's first serial *Ann and Harold* (1938); and regular ballet productions with performances by Margot Fonteyn, Frederick Ashton and Robert Helpmann.

As for outside broadcasts, the medium scored a notable early success with coverage of The Coronation of King George VI (12/5/37), and also transmitted the FA Cup Final of 1938 (30/4/38) and The Test Match against Australia at Lords (1938). Impressive stuff, especially when you consider that *everything* was live, putting enormous pressure on the creative team. A short BBC film *Television Comes To London* (1936) features scenes from the earliest broadcasts, and more importantly *Television Demonstration Film* (1937) recreated on film some examples of the variety of programmes available. The Alexandra Palace Television Archive also has silent colour footage of pre-war rehearsals and some broadcasts, and some private collectors have fragments of programmes on film. And that's it. That's the only record we have of the three early years of television. Hundreds of hours of programmes beamed into the ozone and immediately gone.

Telerecording and videotape

When television returned after the war, the story was much the same; there was still no adequate method of recording live television. (That is not to say there were no repeats. The cost of expensive sets and costumes for plays was often offset by having the entire cast return a few days later to re-stage the play.) But in 1948 the BBC launched *BBC Television Newsreel* and started making its own 35mm film footage of events that could be stored and reused; the first hint of a potential archive. The year before, technicians had finally discovered a way of filming the television screen so that the transmitted image could be kept (telerecording), but the early results were very poor and it wasn't until the early 1950s that this became a viable method for storing and rebroadcasting transmitted programmes.

That still didn't mean, however, that transmissions were kept. TV was thought of as an ephemeral medium with no need of a history and the telerecording technique of archiving was rarely used and then mostly for items of outstanding historic interest or for sports and prestigious arts events. A handful of other delights have survived: producer Rudolph Cartier's plays *It Is Midnight, Dr Schweitzer* (1953) and *1984* (1954 – telerecorded on its second staging due to the furore that its first broadcast had caused); the first two episodes of his *Quatermass Experiment* (1953), written by *1984* adapter Nigel Kneale; two episodes of the BBC soap opera *The Grove Family* (1950s); a couple of early *Dixon of Dock Greens*; quiz shows such as *What's My Line?* – but not a whole lot more.

When ITV came along in 1955, they followed a similar policy although the commercial chan-

Dixon of Dock Green:
Jack Warner

nel's penchant for filmed adventure series meant that many of them survived. But even prestige and expensive productions like *Armchair Theatre* and *Sunday Night At The London Palladium* were mostly unrecorded. The invention of videotape in the late 1950s could have led to extensive archiving, but in fact the very technology of videotape worked against such an occurrence. The fact that videotape could be used again (and was extremely expensive at the time) meant that often, once a programme had had its customary repeat, the tape was wiped and used for something else. Throughout the 1960s, despite the video revolution, thousands of hours of valuable programming was either un-recorded or recorded and wiped. *Juke Box Jury, Top Of The Pops*, first super-soap *Emergency – Ward 10* and later soaps *The Newcomers* and *United!*, the 1960s *Till Death Us Do Part*s, *Thank Your Lucky Stars*, are all represented by a handful of episodes in the archives from the hundreds that were transmitted. Many of the programmes that have survived from that era do so not on tape but on 16mm telerecordings. Even after the invention of videotape, 16mm telerecordings were used extensively especially for overseas sales. There was a simple reason for this – many foreign broadcasters were less advanced than the BBC and some didn't

Sunday Night at the London Palladium

have videotaping facilities. Others were on different television standards which would mean costly tape re-formatting (if possible) so film was a much easier option. It is those 16mm telerecordings destined for overseas sales that have proved invaluable in rebuilding the television archives.

Junking

Broadcasts in colour started on BBC in 1967 and ITV in 1969. By the early 1970s colour broadcasting was the norm rather than the exception (the BBC's *Forsyte Saga* in 1967 was the last major production to be made in black and white [b/w]). Expensive colour sets flew out of the shops and the home audience delighted in this extra dimension to their viewing. The coming of colour of course didn't mean that TV companies would cease to broadcast old b/w movies but television itself never enjoyed the same kudos as film and in most quarters it was decided that the days of b/w television were over. It was argued that viewers who had shelled out good money for new colour sets wouldn't want to watch old b/w shows on them. Thus it was believed that many of the b/w recordings kept by the BBC had outlived their usefulness. Also there were the union rules (Equity, Musicians Union and the Writer's Guild) which only allowed a certain number of transmissions within a certain time period before (often costly) contract renegotiation had to take place. Although many foreign broadcasters were still transmitting (and interested in) b/w programming, much of the material had been deemed to have reached its full sales potential and was looked upon as redundant. These factors, allied to the costs of storage, resulted in the decision to junk huge numbers of telerecordings and also to wipe and re-use videotapes. This practice was common to most companies although the BBC demolition (from 1972) caused the worst casualties. At the BBC the policy was to contact the original producers of the material to be junked to make sure they had no objections to the destruction. In practice it seems that this didn't always happen; there are many examples of producers who claim they weren't contacted (or perhaps were on holiday when approached or had left the Corporation). Those that did give their permission were obviously as unaware as their masters of the future value (both commercial and cultural) of such material.

Restoring the archives

Financial inducement has always driven the television companies to keep some of their output. As more countries around the world started television services, so British broadcasters found a secondary market for their wares and some filmed and telerecorded material would be sold for re-transmission abroad. When the home video market demonstrated the potential of selling programmes on tape, the companies were very quick to respond – and it was really only then that they began to realise the enormous worth of the material that had been wiped, junked or just never recorded. Too late. But, to be honest, not as bad as it could have been. Despite the many items lost, the BBC was in fact aware of the importance of keeping some of their output for posterity and from the late 1950s/early 1960s many outstanding programmes and often at least one example episode of a series were kept. Granada Television likewise had a very coherent archiving policy: witness the fact that every episode of *Coronation Street* survives and its early years continue to make money for the company. And since the late 1970s, almost everything transmitted survives – at least when it comes to whole programmes; it's still difficult to find examples of continuity links, weather reports and the like from that period. But this is a vast improvement. There have also been some remarkable recoveries.

It was probably the obsessive fans of *Doctor Who* who first demonstrated that if you looked hard enough for something it just might turn up where you didn't expect to find it. Undaunted by the fact that episodes were absent from the BBC archives, the fans started searching elsewhere: perhaps foreign TV companies that may have shown the series and not junked or returned their copies as requested; or in the hands of the show's old producers and directors who may have kept copies; possibly mis-filed in the BBC's own archive; maybe even in the hands of private collectors who had rescued the shows from being junked. With a few of the supposedly missing episodes of *Doctor Who* turning up, it alerted archivists to the probability that other such items may be out there. TV companies were also involved in the hunt, a more enlightened archiving policy and the re-sale potential of material firing their enthusiasm.

In 1993, in response to this raid for the lost archives, the BFI launched Missing, Believed Wiped (MBW), an initiative designed to form a focus for such activities. To this end they released a list of twenty key missing programmes, that could just possibly exist somewhere. That list, and the explanation for the entries, is reproduced at the end of this chapter. In the years that MBW

Coronation Street: original cast

has been operating some marvellous material has been returned to the National Film and Television Archive (NFTVA) (a copy of the found material is made and the original is returned to the donor). Highlights include a 1960s Woody Allen appearance where he performs some of his stand-up routine (and fights a boxing kangaroo!); missing episodes of *Monty Python* fore-runner *At Last the 1948 Show*; episodes of *Z Cars*, *Steptoe and Son* and *Till Death Us Do Part*; and material featuring Tony Hancock, Terry-Thomas and Adam Faith. Finds have been unearthed by TV companies, private collectors, fan-clubs and foreign broadcasters sorting through their own archives. Material has been found in garages, lofts, cellars, under beds and on one memorable occasion in a Mormon church.

But there's also a lot of material that is rumoured to be around that hasn't been returned. Episodes of *A For Andromeda*, the Beatles on *Juke Box Jury*, missing *Doctor Who*s are all items that are persistently claimed to exist – and supposedly change hands between collectors – but which haven't officially resurfaced. It's not hard to understand why collectors don't want to return items – in their world such material is currency, rarely being passed on for money but often used for bartering. Also there is no reward for returning material, as obviously copyright and ownership remains with the programme-makers. Thus some collectors feel cheated if they return material out of the kindness of their hearts, only to have the TV companies make seemingly huge amounts of money by reshowing the items, or selling them abroad or on video. (This is particularly true of *Doctor Who*, a programme in demand on traditional, satellite and cable television, as well as on video.) Then there is the feeling of superiority that some collectors get knowing that they have something that nobody else has. Despite that, there are still quite a few collectors who altruistically return material to the public domain getting their kudos from the fact that they found something that nobody else could.

Somewhere out there lurks a lot more of the lost heritage of British television.

TWENTY MOST IMPORTANT MISSING PROGRAMMES

(BFI Press release 1993)

Drama
Armchair Theatre: No Tram to Lime Street
(ABC 1959)
Armchair Theatre, ITV's landmark drama
anthology series, drew vast audiences in the
50s and 60s. Some survive, many do not. *No
Tram to Lime Street* by Alun Owen is arguable
the greatest loss.

A Suitable Case for Treatment
(BBC tx 21.10.62)
One of a series of missing plays by David
Mercer. This one was successful enough to be
remade as a feature-film but the original
television play is not in the archives. Directed
by Don Taylor; written by Ian Hendry.

Madhouse on Castle Street
(BBC tx 13.1.63)
Director Philip Saville had seen Bob Dylan
performing in New York and cast him in this
BBC drama as an anarchistic young man –
before Dylan was known in Britain. He also
sang. The number one missing Dylan item
according to many fans.

Message for Posterity
(BBC tx 3.5.67)
Every Dennis Potter play is a TV event these
days but this, along with some other examples
of his early work, has been lost.

Sci-Fi
A for Andromeda
(BBC tx 3.10.61–14.11.61)

This classic BBC sci-fi series was to the 60s
what *Quatermass* was to the 50s. Julie Christie
was discovered for the title role – an alien
intelligence in a beautiful human form. Only
fragments have survived, including the last
5 minutes, although rumours of the existence
of more material abound.

Doctor Who
esp. 'The Tenth Planet' (episode 4)
(BBC tx 29.10.66)
A concentrated effort by fans and programme
archivists has led to the discovery of many
missing *Doctor Who*'s but there's still more to
come. This adventure, featuring the first
appearance by the Cybermen and the
transmutation of the Doctor from William
Hartnell to Patrick Troughton, would be a
great find.

Out of the Unknown (series 3)
(BBC 1969)
Adult sci-fi from the BBC. Recognised
masterworks of the genre from writers such as
Isaac Asimov and Robert Scheckley were
adapted for the small screen. Only one has
survived.

Comedy
The Likely Lads
(BBC 1964–66)
Clement and La Frenais' wonderful scripts
and James Bolam and Rodney Bewes' wide
boy double act are fondly remembered but
key episodes have gone.

On the Margin
(BBC tx 9.11.66–14.12.66)
Alan Bennett's wonderfully whimsical comedy and music show, now sadly absent from the archive shelves.

Till Death Us Do Part
(BBC 1966–75)
The controversial and ultra-successful sit-com from Johnny Speight dragged the sit-com from it's cosy womb into the modern world. Most of the early series' finest moments are AWOL.

Pop
Juke Box Jury
(BBC 1959–67)
Tragic survival rate for this series (only two exist from the 1960s) but the greatest loss is undoubtedly the show where the four Beatles were the panel judges rating their contemporaries, almost drowned out by screaming fans. (tx 7.12.63)

Thank Your Lucky Stars
(ABC 1961–66)
More missing music. *Thank Your Lucky Stars* attracted all the top pop names of the time and gave us Janice 'I'll give it foive' Nicholls.

Light Entertainment
Sunday Night at the London Palladium
(ATV 1955–65)
The well-remembered long-running variety programme set the standard for TV entertainment. Anyone who was anyone appeared on the Palladium but surprisingly few editions of the show are still around.

Opportunity Knocks
(ABC 1956–77)
Once a stalwart of the schedules, talent shows have all but vanished from our screens. Even the genre's flagship *Opportunity Knocks* has hardly survived, despite featuring the first television performances of many top names.

Current Affairs
Moon Landing (July 1969)
Coverage of the first moon landing. The actual NASA footage does, of course, survive but sadly the live commentary by Patrick Moore and James Burke in the BBC studio is lost in space.

News at Ten
(ITN tx 3.7.67)
ITN's revolutionary late night news bulletin still makes the news today as its slot is argued over. That ground-breaking first bulletin, together with many early programmes, is no longer in the archives.

Childrens
A Tale of Two Cities
(BBC 1965) – and several other Sunday serials from the 50s and 60s
Another vital part of the 60s schedules; the Sunday tea-time classic serials. Despite the obvious long-term appeal of the subject matter, some of the stories were wiped.

Soaps
Emergency – Ward 10
(ATV 1957–67)
First of the really modern British soaps, *Emergency–Ward 10* shirked the domesticity of *The Grove Family* and its like and instead concentrated on the life and death dramas of hospital life. A crucial programme from TV history, yet very few survive.

Jazz
Jazz Goes to College
(BBC2 1966–7)
Many stunning performances, including Ben Webster and Coleman Hawkins no longer available for viewing. The greatest loss is the Albert Ayler programme, recorded but never transmitted (too innovative) – and now gone.

Incomplete
The Crucible
(Granada 1959)
Not all programmes have totally vanished. Some, like this version of 'The Crucible' starring Sean Connery and Susannah York exist in part. (Only one 60-min. tape survives – the final 18 mins are missing.) Tracking down missing reels, or combining incomplete copies is another vital undertaking.

MISSING, BELIEVED WIPED – EVENT HISTORY

Programmes that are returned to the archives (whether through the initiative or otherwise) are then available for repeat screenings on TV (à la *The Lost Steptoes*) and/or commercial video/DVD release. Some of the material proves useful for extracts on various TV entertainment/history programmes. The BFI is also committed to showing returned material, and to that end a major part of MBW has been the regular screenings of material at the NFT in London. There follows a breakdown of the many MBW events with details of the material screened.

1993

Saturday 2nd October at the NFT
Barry Took introduced the entire event commenting on the worth of some of the missing programmes and extending his hopes that this initiative may result in the recovery of some valuable lost material.

The first event consisted of a number of on-stage sessions looking at different aspects of MBW.

The search goes on: rediscovering treasures
Steve Bryant (Keeper of Television, NFTVA), Adam Lee (Archive Selector, BBC) and Tony Rowlands (ex Thames TV) presented the story of recovering missing material.

Screening (Programme One)
A For Andromeda – Opening titles and recently rediscovered final five minutes of the last episode. (BBC 14.11.61)
Cilla – Brief extract (3 mins) from *Cilla in Berlin* once thought lost but recently returned to the BBC by the European partners who had co-produced the programme. (BBC 20.11.71)
Doctor Who: Ambassadors of Death (episode 5) – Extract (6 mins) from classic sci-fi adventure. (BBC 18.4.70)

Till Death Us Do Part: 'Peace and Goodwill' – Directly as a result of MBW, a collector contacted the BFI and allowed us to copy this 17-minute surviving section from a Christmas Special edition of the famous sitcom. (BBC 26.12.66)
The New London Palladium Show – Recovered by the Independent Television Commission (ITC) this was a true oddity. Sir Lew Grade had borrowed some 525 line US cameras to film (in colour!) some editions of his famous Palladium shows. A rare colour record of a landmark British TV series. Extract (13 mins) featuring, top of the bill, Roy Orbison. (ATV 20.3.66)

Restoring the picture – the technical challenge
Technicians Brian Jenkinson (NFTVA) and Ralph Montagu (BBC) highlighted the difficult and varied problems associated with treating old material, some of which survives on sub-standard formats in dubious condition.

Rescuing pop or how did *Juke Box Jury* end up in the US
Music researchers/aficionados John Platt, Andy Neil and Keith Badman discussed the peculiar problems (and advantages) of tracking down missing TV music items.

Where Do We Go From Here?
Steve Bryant looked at the future possibilities for recovering missing programmes.

Screening (Programme Two)
Moonbase 3 – This part sci-fi/part soap series was long missing from the BBC archives, but diligent work by BBC archivists located copies in the US and all six parts were returned to the UK. We screened Episode 1: *Departure and Arrival* (9.9.73) and Episode 6: *Views of a Dead Planet* (14.10.73).

1994

Saturday 1st October at the NFT
The most lucrative source of recovered material that resulted from the original MBW launch was a collection of 16mm telerecordings held by a private collector, Harold Barney, who had had the material for over twenty years. This material made up the bulk of the screenings in this second MBW event.

Introduced as usual by Steve Bryant, this session ended in spectacular fashion with an impromptu (and hilarious) summation from guest Bob Monkhouse, an acknowledged authority in the field of variety and known himself to be a collector of TV and film material.

Screenings
Barney Collection:
At Last the 1948 Show – An original edition of the famous ITV comedy sketch show that was an important stepping stone on the way to *Monty Python's Flying Circus*. 25 mins (Rediffusion 8.3.67)
Hippodrome – A British circus/variety programme introduced by guest host Woody Allen and featuring the comedian's stand-up act and an unforgettable

Comedy Playhouse: 'The Old Campaigner' – Terry-Thomas and Derek Fowlds

sequence in which he goes into the ring with a real-life boxing kangaroo. 50 mins (Rediffusion 10.10.66)
Comedy Playhouse: 'The Old Campaigner' – Original pilot for series featuring comedy superstar Terry-Thomas typically cast as a quick-talking rogue with an eye for the ladies and a nose for a quick buck. 25 mins (BBC 30.6.67)
Seven Deadly Sins – Extract (30 mins) from episode of anthology series on the theme of the Seven Deadly Sins. This segment featured pop star Adam Faith in an early acting role. (Rediffusion 13.6.66)
No, That's Me Over Here! – Episode of famous Ronnie Corbett sitcom written by Barry Cryer and Graham Chapman. 25 mins (Rediffusion 1967/68)
Also featured:
Till Death Us Do Part: 'The Polls' – Special election day episode from the famous sitcom. (BBC 18.6.70)
Hancock's Half Hour – Surviving 5-minute segment from Tony Hancock's ABC series (his last in Britain). (30.6.67).
Both these items were recovered by collector Terry Martini who specialises in tracking

down missing items that survive on early domestic videotape.

Dave Cash Radio Programme – Colourful, wacky pop programme discovered (on film) at a movie jumble and purchased for the NFTVA. (HTV 1972).

Off The Record – Early pop programme. Extract (3 mins) featuring singer Max Bygraves. (BBC 1955)

New Faces – Comedy great Victoria Wood featured in this recently rediscovered extract (7 mins) from the famous talent spotting show. (ATV/ITC 1974) Returned by comedian/host Les Dennis.

Doctor Who: The Dalek Master Plan (Episode 3: *Devil's Planet*) – Ephemeral seconds from missing *Doctor Who* episode found lurking in the *Blue Peter* archives. (BBC 20.11.65)

1995

Sunday 22nd October at the NFT

The whole event in this year was given over to one remarkable find. Jon Keeble, the ATV/ITC archivist (at that time), unearthed a whole Sunday evening of ITV that had been recorded by Sir Lew Grade. This was a complete evening with programmes, continuity, adverts, promos, news reports, etc. A unique opportunity to recall an evening of 1960s television exactly as it went out. Some of these programmes may well have survived separately, but in the context of the whole evening it was certainly material MBW.

Screening

The ITV Sunday night schedule from 22nd March 1964

About Religion – Well-known actors read moving passages from classic and contemporary poetry and prose. (A-R)

77 Sunset Strip: Your Fortune For A Penny – Robert Vaughn guest stars in an episode from the classic US private detective series.

Sunday Night at the London Palladium – Bruce Forsyth hosts the famous variety series, this week featuring wacky popsters Freddie and the Dreamers. (ATV)

Studio 64: Happy Moorings – Keith Waterhouse and Willis Hall comedy drama about divorce starring Roy Kinnear and Millicent Martin. (ATV)

The October special TV event for 1996 concentrated on BBC TV's 60th anniversary, and the 1997 event was a historical overview of colour broadcasting in the UK. MBW returned in 1998.

1998

Saturday 17th October 1998 at the NFT

Private collectors were responsible for the bulk of 1998's screenings. The programme notes thanked the following: Brian Sammes, Andrew Henderson, Andrew Doherty, Andrew Emmerson, Dick Fiddy, Stella Richman, Brian Taylor, Harold Barney, Ray Galton, Alan Simpson, Tessa Le Bars, Neil Ingoe and John Aspinall.

The second programme of screenings was specially introduced by actor Frank Windsor, who appeared in two of the returned shows *Half Hour Story: Robert* (screened in Programme One) and *Z Cars: Contraband*.

This year was also notable for the forging of closer ties with Andrew Emmerson and Andrew Henderson, who are part of the team responsible for putting together *405 Alive*, a magazine for television nostalgists (see Reference section). They have had a long history of tracking down missing and obscure television items and over the following years would contribute some outstanding items to the MBW events.

Z Cars: Frank Windsor

Screening (Programme One)

BBC News Bulletin – A whole news bulletin from the late 1950s, read by Robert Dougall. A fascinating glimpse of the news telling techniques of the time. Returned by Andrew Doherty. (BBC 26.2.58)

Cool for Cats – Innovative pop show compered (mainly) by Kent Walton, later best known as the voice of wrestling. Recent releases were played (occasionally with the artists miming along) and a regular team of (highly energetic) dancers would interpret the music. This edition was filmed as an attempt to sell the format of the show to the US, and is the only record of the show. Kent Walton and some of the series' original dancers were in the NFT audience to witness this rare treat. (A-R 1958)

Ideal Home – A special edition of the UK's most popular ever advertising magazine (admag) *Jim's Inn*. Admags were short programmes featuring regular characters and/or personalities who introduced viewers to various products. *Jim's Inn*, starring comedy actor Jimmy Hanley, successfully combined soap opera sensibilities with direct sales talk and was fondly remembered by a generation of viewers. No editions were thought to have survived (although some were rumoured to be in the hands of private collectors) until this special surfaced. (A-R 7.3.61)

Object Z: The Meteor – From the Harold Barney collection, donated due to the publicity surrounding the first MBW event. *Object Z* was a sci-fi series about a huge meteor heading towards the Earth. This was the opening episode; the rest of the series has subsequently been rediscovered within the NFTVA collection. (Rediffusion 19.10.65)

Big Night Out: The Peggy Lee Show – *Big Night Out* was one of the many lavish ITV variety series. In this extract singer Peggy Lee performs her famous hit 'Fever'. Donated by Andrew Henderson. (ABC tx unknown)

Object Z

Half Hour Story: Robert – Ridley Scott
directed this segment of the Associated
Rediffusion short drama strand. Returned
by the producer Stella Richman.
(Rediffusion 2.8.67)

Steptoe and Son: 'Men of Property' – Last of
the so-called Lost Steptoes, this episode
was actually on the very first Steptoe tape
returned to the NFTVA, but was not
restored until just prior to this screening.
(BBC 17.4.70)

Screening (Programme Two)

Big Night Out: The Peggy Lee Show – Second
extract from this show features Peggy Lee
in a musical sketch set in a waxworks
museum. One of the models turns out to
be the real Bing Crosby making an
unscheduled (and uncredited) cameo
appearance. (ABC tx unknown)

Fabian of the Yard: Robbery at the Museum –
Famous early detective series based on the
real-life exploits of celebrated Scotland
Yard detective Robert Fabian. Donated by
John Aspinall. (BBC 11.5.55)

Murder Bag – Early ITV cop series which
introduced Francis Lockhart (played by
Raymond Francis), a dour, snuff-taking cop
of the old school. Lockart would also
appear in the series *Crime Sheet* before
getting his most famous vehicle, the highly
rated *No Hiding Place*. The Murder Bag of
the title was the police kit taken to the scene
of a killing. ATV archivist Brian Sammes
unearthed this segment which featured two
different title sequences (as the series
sometime reverted to *Crime Bag* when the
crime in question wasn't murder). Also –
oddly – it doesn't feature Raymond Francis,
as the pre-credit voice over explains that the
actor is 'unwell this week' and is replaced by
another actor! (A-R tx unknown)

Mark Saber: The Sucker Game – Complicated
title differences meant that this series was
known by various names, but was most
famous as *Mark Saber* or *The Vise*. Donald
Grey played the one-armed private
detective Mark Saber: Grey himself had
lost an arm in the war. This episode
featured a young Michael Caine. (A-R
6.5.58)

Z Cars: Contraband – Fine episode of the
classic cop series that changed forever the
on-screen depiction of the police. This
story centred on ambitious uniformed
officer Fancy Smith (Brian Blessed) and
his attempts to impress the CID. (BBC
28.6.62)

1999

Saturday 30th October 1999 at the NFT
Private collectors again provided the bulk of
returned material for this screening, especially
Andrew Emmerson and Andrew Henderson.

Screening (Programme One)
Donated by Andrew Emmerson:

Robin Hood: The Abbot of St Mary – Only
surviving episode of early BBC Robin
Hood serial with Patrick Troughton as the
altruistic outlaw. (24.3.53)

Rats to You – Extract from showbiz charity
Water Rats variety show, featuring Max
Bygraves, with wooden superstar Archie
Andrews. (BBC 1956)

Setting Up Home – Admag featuring (among
others) a young Geoffrey Palmer. (ATV 1959)

From the BBC

Cinderella – The BBC's Ralph Montagu
introduced a clip from this recently
rediscovered TV pantomime. The extract
featured Beryl Reid and Jack Tripp as the
Ugly Sisters. (BBC 25.12.69)

Donated by Andrew Henderson

Mogul: Wildcat – Episode of the famous oil
business drama series Mogul which later
changed its name to *The Troubleshooters*. This
episode dealt with racism. (BBC 28.7.65)

From the BBC

Dusty – Sue Malden (of BBC archives)
introduced a recently returned edition of
Dusty Springfield's acclaimed 1960s series.
Veteran ventriloquist Señor Wences was
the guest star. (BBC 22.9.66)

Donated by Andrew Emmerson

Pre-war Transmission – A truly remarkable find.
In 1938 RCA TV engineers in upstate New
York were puzzled by signals they were
receiving on their equipment. It soon
dawned on them that these must be BBC
transmissions amazingly travelling
thousands of miles because of sun spot
activity and freak atmospheric conditions.
Broadcasts from Alexandra Palace only
travelled 30 miles or so at the time, but in
this unique case they were being bounced
off the ionosphere and picked up thousands
of miles away on the American East Coast.
The engineers retuned their equipment to
collect the signals more clearly and one of
their number filmed the resulting images.
Rumours of the film's existence circulated
for many years but the film itself never
seemed to surface. TV enthusiast Andy
Emmerson tried for years to track it down
but without success … until a friend at the
American Vintage Wireless Collectors
Society agreed to mention it in their
magazine. Andy Emmerson was contacted
by Maurice Schecheter, who worked in the
industry. He had a collection of television
material *including* the RCA recordings on
16mm film. The material was cleaned up
digitally and a copy sent to Andy

Emmerson. Its first public display was as
part of the reopening ceremony at the
refurbished National Museum of
Photography, Film and TV in Bradford in
June 1999. The film shows a few minutes of
spooky images rolling and tumbling before
becoming stable for a few tantalising
seconds every now and then. Certain faces
(early announcer Jasmine Bligh for one) are
recognisable – much is not. But the effect of
the film is undeniable and it rates as the
most amazing scientific and historic item
ever shown (so far) at a MBW event.

Screening (Programme Two)

Donated by Andrew Henderson

Sprat Fishing – Marvellous example of the type
of 'filler' mini-documentaries to be found
on TV in the 1950s and early 1960s. Sprat
Fishing looks at all aspects of the industry
from catching the fish to canning and
distribution. A simple but well-made and
highly watchable item. (ATV tx unknown)

BBC OB – Extract from early BBC outside
broadcast of a military display attended by
royalty. (BBC 1950s)

Just the Job – Another one of the admags
which, at one time, seemed like an
endangered species, but which now exist
in healthy numbers thanks to MBW. This
one was hosted by radio funny man
Kenneth Horne who also features in the
next item. (A-R 1950s)

From the BBC

Rehearsal clips – The BBC's Ralph Montagu
introduced this rare find of rehearsal
footage for Kenneth Horne's ITV show
Horne a Plenty. Nothing of the series
proper survives but these colour segments
at least offer an insight into the look and
style of the programme. The BBC's Paul

Vanezis was responsible for the recovery of this material (at BBC Birmingham): a perfect example of the fact that missing programmes often turn up in the wrong archive or with the wrong broadcaster. (Thames rehearsal for show transmitted 25.12.68)

Donated by Edward Joffe
Your Shopping Service – Extract from an admag donated by film editor Edward Joffe, who at the time, had worked for the company that made various admags. This one starred Barbara Kelly. (ITV – company unknown – c. 1956)

Presented by Chris Perry of Kaleidoscope
The Likely Lads: 'Last of the Big Spenders' – A missing episode of the classic BBC TV comedy series (tx 7.7.65). This film was in the hands of a collector who had it for sale. The negotiations to purchase were quite delicate and were handled by enthusiast and collector Neil Ingoe. Ingoe finally bought the episode (on behalf of Kaleidoscope) and we screened a 5-minute extract from the programme prior to its presentation in full at the next Kaleidoscope screening event. Following that screening the episode was returned to the BBC.

Presented by Sue Malden of the BBC
Archivist Sue Malden introduced a complete edition of a 1970s *Top of the Pops* (22.6.72) recently returned to the BBC archive.

Donated by Andrew Henderson
Boyd QC – Complete episode from classic British drama series following the cases of barrister Richard Boyd, smoothly played by veteran British screen actor Michael Denison.

2000
Saturday 2nd December at the NFT
A real mixed bunch this time with some more material from the very early days of TV.

Screening (Programme One)
From the Alexandra Palace TV Archive
Pre- and Post-War Colour Footage from Ally Pally – A remarkable find by the Alexandra Palace Archive introduced by Steven Vaughn. This was 20 minutes of remarkable, colour 16mm film shot at the BBC's Alexandra Palace studios in the 1930s and 1940s. The film was shot by cameraman D. R. Campbell and for many years had been stored in a shed at his home. It was donated by his daughter. Sadly there had been many more hours of this material but a fire some years earlier had claimed quite a bit. However, the material that survives is breathtaking. So little from that period survives anyway, but to have a colour record of how the service operated at that time is invaluable. Lots of studio shots, clips of equipment and tantalising fragments of full dress rehearsals and some actual shows.

From Edward Joffe
Australian Tony Hancock Show Colour Rehearsal Footage – Edward Joffe, who was the director on Tony Hancock's (aborted) Australian series, kept this colour footage showing Hancock in rehearsal. This is virtually the last footage ever shot of Hancock, and although it shows the comic as a shadow of his earlier self, it still contains flashes of genius to remind you of his undeniable greatness.
(Extract 10 mins)

Donated by Maurice Kanarek

It's A Knockout Trailer – Director Maurice Kanarek, who shot many TV trailers, introduced this oddity, a specially shot promo (pitched as a Western) for the BBC's famous fun and games competition *It's A Knockout*. (2 mins)

From the BBC

Aladdin and His Wonderful Lamp – One of a trio of BBC TV (25.12.66) pantomimes that resurfaced at one of the regional BBC stations. This one featured Anita Harris and Roy Castle, but was stolen by the old trooper Arthur Askey as Widow Twanky. (Extract 5 mins)

Harry Worth: 'James Bond Where Are You' – A bunch of Harry Worth episodes from this period (1966–70) were returned to the BBC archive. This episode (18.11.70) followed the hapless comedian as he accidentally got involved in some international intrigue.

Screening (Programme 2)

Donated by Edward Joffe

Talking Shop – Another of the admags, once so rare, but now returned to the archive in some numbers thanks to MBW. Donated by director Edward Joffe.

Donated by Harold Barney

Television Playhouse: A Builder by Trade – This was recovered way back in the early days of MBW and was part of the cachement of 16mm telerecordings returned by Harold Barney. This film had no opening and closing credits and it was only earlier in 2000 that Kathleen Luckey, one of the BFI's researchers, discovered which drama it actually was. This is a well-acted, absorbing drama which looks at aspirations, romance and class. It starred Michael Williams and was originally transmitted by A-R on 15.2.63.

Donated by Mike Wormersley

Freewheelers: Menace (Episode 5: *Face to Face*) – Mike Wormersley, the original film editor on *Freewheelers*, thankfully saved many episodes of the cult action/adventure series for younger viewers, described as a juvenile James Bond series. The previous year the NFT had screened an entire adventure from the *Freewheelers* series (courtesy of Mike), with some of the original cast present. Here we included the final episode of the very first adventure to publicise this return. (Southern Television 2.5.68)

Freewheelers: Geoffrey Toone

From the NFTVA

Larry Grayson – Extract from the camp
comedian's own show.

Ev – Early (1970) series featuring madcap disc
jockey Kenny Everett in what seems in
many ways a TV version of his popular
radio show, complete with musical guest
stars and primitive forms of the pop video.
This compilation edition came to light
because of the Heritage Lottery Fund,
which is providing finance for the NFTVA
to transfer old 2-inch tapes onto digibeta.

From Mark Lewisohn

Thank Your Lucky Stars On Merseyside – A
special Mersey edition of *Thank Your
Lucky Stars* featuring Gerry and the
Pacemakers, The Searchers and The
Beatles. This edition – officially missing –
was known to be available on the
collectors' market in the US and this VHS
copy was donated by media writer Mark
Lewisohn. We screened it in the hope that
the surrounding publicity may lead to the
return of a better quality copy – perhaps
even a master. (ABC 21.12.63)

CASE STUDY 1: *AT LAST THE 1948 SHOW*

In a continental coastal bar sit four self-made Yorkshiremen, each trying to outdo each other with stories of their bleak, poverty stricken upbringing ('There were 150 of us living in a shoe-box in t'middle of road' 'Cardboard box?' 'Aye' 'You were lucky!'). This classic sketch was a high-light of the *Monty Python Live at Drury Lane* album (and later the charity comedy bash *The Secret Policeman's Ball*), and has since become a firm favourite with fans. The sketch had a famil-iar feel and many viewers erroneously supposed it to be from *Monty Python's Flying Circus* (remember this was before endless repeats and pre-recorded video availability re-acquainted fans with every word of the Python scripts), but actually the sketch first aired on TV as part of *At Last the 1948 Show*, a Rediffusion anarchic comedy series that was an important stepping stone on the way to *Monty Python*.

The future Python team (apart from Terry Gilliam) had all worked (in separate writing teams) for *The Frost Report* (BBC), David Frost's theme-based sketch and monologue series which began in 1966. Frost greatly admired the work of John Cleese and suggested that Cleese might like to

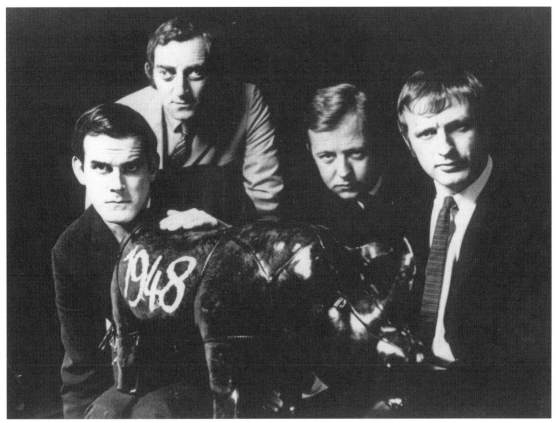

At Last the 1948 Show: John Cleese, Marty Feldman, Tim Brooke-Taylor and Graham Chapman.

join forces with another of the series writers, Tim Brooke-Taylor and create a new series which Frost would produce independently and sell to the ITV network. Cleese went along with the idea and his writing partner Graham Chapman was naturally added to the mix. Marty Feldman – a veteran radio and TV writer who with his partner Barry Took had created the marvellous wireless hit *Round the Horne* – had been one of the chief writers on *The Frost Report* and Cleese suggested that he also be brought on board. At first Frost was unsure, mainly because of Feldman's weird pop-eyed looks, the result of an operation he'd had in the early 1960s for a severe hyperthyroid condition. Cleese however convinced Frost, and later Frost would champion Feldman when trying to sell the series to Rediffusion.

At Last the 1948 Show – the title of a Cleese joke relating to the length of time it took to get an idea into production – debuted (in the London area) on 15th February 1967 and presented a rapid paced mix of unrelated manic sketches, most featuring a surreal occasionally violent edge, hitherto rarely seen on TV. The show was linked by 'the lovely Aimi MacDonald', a gold-digging dumb blonde who believed it to be her show. Actress Aimi MacDonald expertly played dense, exaggerating her Betty Boop style voice and appearing in a number of risqué glamorous outfits, offering a neat contrast to the male-heavy sketches (all acted by the four team members with occasional assistance from Bill Oddie, Barry Cryer, Dick Vosburgh and Eric Idle).

As with *Python,* the team members created, wrote and performed the material which was remarkably close in style to that which would later be described as Pythonesque. The programme had a chequered history, but lasted for two series: the first, six episodes, the second seven. Some ITV stations didn't take it at all, others just aired one series (ATV only screened series 1, Granada only series 2). But in the London area the show was a big hit, making the top ten for the region. Although not as accomplished as the later *Python*, the series nevertheless had its moments. The liberal format offered great freedom to the writer/performers who were able to fully exploit their weird ideas. The series featured wonderful sketches which were sadly let down by some poor punchlines – it was the introduction of overlapping sketches and animation links which enabled *Python* to move away from punchlines and towards something completely different.

So, why isn't *At Last the 1948 Show* regularly repeated, or available on DVD or video? The sad fact is that eleven of the thirteen episodes were wiped soon after they were made – a victim of the economy drives which caused much material to be erased in order to reuse the tapes (which were hugely expensive at the time). Two episodes survived in the NFTVA, a small taster of an important series. For many years that was thought to be it.

In 1989 I was working as a writer/researcher on Channel 4's New Year's Day archive celebration *The A to Z of TV*, a 3-hour extravaganza looking back at the history of British TV. One of the researchers, John Platt, an acknowledged authority on pop and rock acts' appearances on TV, had discovered that a lot of UK TV material from that field had survived in Sweden and he suggested I talk to them about what other types of UK programming they might have. I discovered that they had the famous 'Four Yorkshiremen' sketch, long thought lost from the *1948 Show*. We managed to get the sketch back from Sweden and presented it as part of *The A to Z of TV*. This screening alerted certain aficionados who knew that the sketch was officially missing. I spoke to Steve Bryant, Keeper of Television at the BFI, and told him of the Swedish connection. Bryant called his contacts at Swedish Television, archivists Sten Frykholm and Lasse Nilsson, and they confirmed that they held five episodes of *At Last the 1948 Show*s. These were 16mm telerecordings (a traditional format for overseas sales) which they had kept since the 1960s. Bryant arranged for the material to be shipped back to the UK to be viewed. The big question now was whether these were five brand new episodes or whether they duplicated any of the two already surviving in the archive. The answer was a complete surprise.

The five Swedish episodes turned out to be compilations culled from all thirteen editions of *At Last the 1948 Show*. Obviously the material that would work best internationally had been isolated and re-edited into these new editions. Although this provided a valuable record of some of the show's sketches it didn't show the careful structure of the original productions which could be seen in the surviving two episodes in the archive (later there would be a third episode, returned to the NFTVA by a private collector – Harold Barney – in the mid-1990s).

There the story may have ended if it wasn't for Ray Frensham. Today, Ray Frensham is a successful writer/broadcaster whose *Teach Yourself Screenwriting* book has sent many a budding film scribe on their way. But in 1967 Frensham was a callow teenager obsessed by the radio programme *I'm Sorry I'll Read That Again* (ISIRTA), which starred, among others, John Cleese and Tim Brooke-Taylor (and where in fact the famous 'Four Yorkshiremen' sketch was first performed). For Christmas 1964 he had been given a Philips reel-to-reel tape recorder and he set about taping and keeping every edition of ISIRTA, as well as attending many of the recordings in person. He also kept tabs on individual appearances by members of the ISIRTA team and to this end actually recorded off-air all thirteen editions of *At Last the 1948 Show*. Not only that but, unlike many of his tele-taping contemporaries Frensham dutifully logged all his recordings and kept them in pristine condition.

Spin forward over twenty-five years: Frensham was interviewing Steve Bryant for an article in *The Stage* newspaper and mentioned that he still had these audio copies. This gave Bryant the germ of the idea that, with these audio tapes, it would be possible to reconstruct some of the lost editions of the series. Some years later the fruits of their collaboration saw the light of day (Premiered at the NFT's annual television festival TV2000 in Sept 2000). Frensham's audio recordings (of surprisingly good quality) were transferred onto digibeta tapes and combined with the surviving visual material from the Swedish compilations (also transferred to digibeta) to make new copies of two *1948 Show* editions. The results are tapes which restore the continuity of the original broadcasts – albeit with certain parts of each programme existing only as sound material played over a still photograph of the sketch, or the relevant pages of the original script. Nevertheless the overall effect is undeniably rewarding, offering a once-believed-impossible chance to experience again two editions of an important and hilarious TV comedy series long thought to be Missing, Believed Wiped.

CASE STUDY 2: *DOCTOR WHO*

Millions of words have been written about *Doctor Who* and many of these have dealt with the issue of missing episodes. Here is an overview looking at the partial destruction and gradual reconstruction of a TV legend.

By the mid- to late 1970s the sci-fi series *Doctor Who* had transcended its earlier manifestation as a fantasy romp for younger viewers (albeit with a cultish appeal) to become a hugely popular institution enjoyed by a new generation of fans and also maintaining a percentage of older fans who had grown up with the series. It also had a considerable fan base abroad in territories where the series had been sold. With an ever-expanding international market for such material and with the fledgeling domestic video market demonstrating the potential of such cult material to avid fans, the BBC were sitting on an archive goldmine – or should have been. As with many of its contemporaries, huge amounts of *Doctor Who* had been junked in the BBC's wiping campaign of a few years earlier (the details of this policy and the thinking behind it were discussed

Doctor Who: Wendy Padbury, Patrick Troughton and Frazer Hines

in the 'Background' chapter). The result was that some 200 episodes of the series were thought to be totally missing.

In 1978 the BBC officially set up its videotape and film archive, and BBC archivist Sue Malden chose *Doctor Who* as an example to explore the BBC's previous archival policy and its effect on BBC holdings. She set about gauging the extent of the losses and, where possible, looked elsewhere for missing episodes. Many initially turned up in the BBC Enterprises Sales Vault (although some of these were b/w 16mm telerecordings of episodes originally broadcast in colour) and were absorbed into the Film and Videotape Library. Still some 146 episodes were totally absent. Now, over twenty years later, only 109 episodes are missing. The recovered material has come from a number of different sources and highlights the serendipitous nature of this type of treasure hunt. Foreign archives, home video recordings, car boot sales, private collectors, the NFTVA (then known as the NFA), production staff (engineers, etc.) and, most bizarrely, the cellar of a Mormon church, have all yielded missing episodes and helped fill some of the blanks.

Doctor Who fan Ian Levine was a pioneer in the quest to retrieve the missing episodes and his enthusiasm for the project resulted in crucial leads and valuable finds. This unofficial alliance between fans and archivists, both from the BBC and beyond, has shown how a dedicated effort can produce results.

But what of those last lost 109 episodes? Some are rumoured to exist in the hands of private collectors but actual numbers are debatable here – such collectors' markets are fuelled by rumour and optimistic expectation. What is known, however, is that audio recordings of all 109 do exist. It transpired many fans had audio recorded episodes off-air, although the quality of such recordings varied. But amongst these amateur archivists were a couple who had recordings of breathtaking clarity. Graham Strong was one such who had wired his tape deck up to his TV and had audio copies of marvellous quality. A large number of stills (including 'telesnaps' shots taken of TV screens) also existed for the missing episodes and these have been combined with the audio recordings to create an audio/visual reminder of the lost episodes. Fans organised these restoration combinations initially, but later the BBC themselves started to release the audio recordings.

Here is a list of the 109 episodes still missing:

DOCTOR WHO – MISSING EPISODES

Story name: episode name	episode number	story number	tx date
Marco Polo: Roof Of The World	1	D	22/2/64
Marco Polo: Singing Sands	2	D	29/2/64
Marco Polo: Five Hundred Eyes	3	D	7/3/64
Marco Polo: Walls Of Lies	4	D	14/3/64
Marco Polo: Rider From Shang-Tu	5	D	21/3/64
Marco Polo: Mighty Kublai Khan	6	D	28/3/64
Marco Polo: Assassin At Peking	7	D	4/4/64

Story name: episode name	episode number	story number	tx date
The Reign Of Terror: Tyrant Of France	4	H	29/8/64
The Reign Of Terror: A Bargain Of Necessity	5	H	5/9/64
The Crusade: Knights Of Jaffa	2	P	3/4/65
The Crusade: The Warlords	4	P	17/4/65
Galaxy Four: Four Hundred Dawns	1	T	11/9/65
Galaxy Four: Trap Of Steel	2	T	18/9/65
Galaxy Four: Air Lock	3	T	25/9/65
Galaxy Four: Exploding Planet	4	T	2/10/65
Mission To The Unknown	1	T/A	9/10/65
The Myth Makers: Temple Of Secrets	1	U	16/10/65
The Myth Makers: Small Prophet Quick Return	2	U	23/10/65
The Myth Makers: Death Of A Spy	3	U	30/10/65
The Myth Makers: Horse Of Destruction	4	U	6/11/65
The Daleks' Master Plan: The Nightmare Begins	1	V	13/11/65
The Daleks' Master Plan: Day Of Armageddon	2	V	20/11/65
The Daleks' Master Plan: Devil's Planet	3	V	27/11/65
The Daleks' Master Plan: The Traitors	4	V	4/12/65
The Daleks' Master Plan: Coronas Of The Sun	6	V	18/12/65
The Daleks' Master Plan: Feast Of Steven	7	V	25/12/65
The Daleks' Master Plan: Volcano	8	V	1/1/66
The Daleks' Master Plan: Golden Death	9	V	8/1/66
The Daleks' Master Plan: Abandoned Planet	11	V	22/1/66
The Daleks' Master Plan: Destruction Of Time	12	V	29/1/66
The Massacre: War Of God	1	W	5/2/66
The Massacre: Sea Beggar	2	W	12/2/66
The Massacre: Priest Of Death	3	W	19/2/66
The Massacre: Bell Of Doom	4	W	26/2/66
The Celestial Toymaker: Celestial Toyroom	1	X	2/4/66
The Celestial Toymaker: Hall Of Dolls	2	X	9/4/66
The Celestial Toymaker: Dancing Floor	3	X	16/4/66
The Savages	1	AA	28/5/66
The Savages	2	AA	4/6/66
The Savages	3	AA	11/6/66
The Savages	4	AA	18/6/66
The Smugglers	1	CC	10/9/66
The Smugglers	2	CC	17/9/66
The Smugglers	3	CC	24/9/66
The Smugglers	4	CC	1/10/66
The Tenth Planet	4	DD	29/10/66
Power Of The Daleks	1	EE	5/11/66

Story name: episode name	episode number	story number	tx date
Power Of The Daleks	2	EE	12/11/66
Power Of The Daleks	3	EE	22/11/66
Power Of The Daleks	4	EE	29/11/66
Power Of The Daleks	5	EE	3/12/66
Power Of The Daleks	6	EE	10/12/66
The Highlanders	1	FF	17/12/66
The Highlanders	2	FF	24/12/66
The Highlanders	3	FF	31/12/66
The Highlanders	4	FF	7/1/67
The Underwater Menace	1	GG	14/1/67
The Underwater Menace	2	GG	21/1/67
The Underwater Menace	4	GG	4/2/67
The Moonbase	1	HH	11/2/67
The Moonbase	3	HH	25/2/67
The Macra Terror	1	JJ	11/3/67
The Macra Terror	2	JJ	18/3/67
The Macra Terror	3	JJ	25/3/67
The Macra Terror	4	JJ	1/4/67
The Faceless Ones	2	KK	15/4/67
The Faceless Ones	4	KK	29/4/67
The Faceless Ones	5	KK	6/5/67
The Faceless Ones	6	KK	13/5/67
The Evil Of The Daleks	1	LL	20/5/67
The Evil Of The Daleks	3	LL	3/6/67
The Evil Of The Daleks	4	LL	10/6/67
The Evil Of The Daleks	5	LL	17/6/67
The Evil Of The Daleks	6	LL	24/6/67
The Evil Of The Daleks	7	LL	1/8/67
The Abominable Snowmen	1	NN	30/9/67
The Abominable Snowmen	3	NN	14/10/67
The Abominable Snowmen	4	NN	21/10/67
The Abominable Snowmen	5	NN	28/10/67
The Abominable Snowmen	6	NN	4/11/67
The Ice Warriors	2	OO	18/11/67
The Ice Warriors	3	OO	25/11/67
The Enemy Of The World	1	PP	23/12/67
The Enemy Of The World	2	PP	30/12/67
The Enemy Of The World	4	PP	13/1/68
The Enemy Of The World	5	PP	20/1/68
The Enemy Of The World	6	PP	27/1/68

Story name: episode name	episode number	story number	tx date
The Web Of Fear	2	QQ	10/2/68
The Web Of Fear	3	QQ	17/2/68
The Web Of Fear	4	QQ	24/2/68
The Web Of Fear	5	QQ	2/3/68
The Web Of Fear	6	QQ	9/3/68
Fury From The Deep	1	RR	16/3/68
Fury From The Deep	2	RR	23/3/68
Fury From The Deep	3	RR	30/3/68
Fury From The Deep	4	RR	6/4/68
Fury From The Deep	5	RR	13/4/68
Fury From The Deep	6	RR	20/4/68
The Wheel In Space	1	SS	27/4/68
The Wheel In Space	2	SS	4/5/68
The Wheel In Space	4	SS	18/5/68
The Wheel In Space	5	SS	25/5/68
The Invasion	1	VV	2/11/68
The Invasion	4	VV	23/11/68
The Space Pirates	1	YY	8/3/69
The Space Pirates	3	YY	22/3/69
The Space Pirates	4	YY	29/3/69
The Space Pirates	5	YY	5/4/69
The Space Pirates	6	YY	12/4/69

NOTE: Up to and including 'The Ark' (story Y) each episode had its own title. Any film can containing an episode from this period is more likely to have the episode title than the story name. The captions on the episode opening feature the episode name only, although in some cases, the name of the first episode is the also the name of the story!

CASE STUDY 3: *THE LOST STEPTOES*

In the 1980s it was known that fourteen episodes of *Steptoe and Son*, arguably Britain's greatest ever sitcom, were lost. One episode was from the original 1960s b/w run ('My Old Man's A Tory', tx 8.11.65) the others were from the first two colour series in 1970. In 1989, I chatted to writers Ray Galton and Alan Simpson in the offices of their representative Tessa Le Bars, discussing various things including a possible NFT event. The conversation got around to the missing *Steptoe* episodes and Ray mentioned that he had some domestic videotape recordings of some of these shows. These had been done for his own personal use on a half-inch monochrome open reel machine. I expressed an interest in seeing this material and, because Ray no longer had a working machine to play them on, he gave me one of the tapes. I sought out a BBC engineer who had

Steptoe and Son: Harry H. Corbett and Wilfrid Brambell

Steptoe and Son: 'My Old Man's a Tory', Harry H. Corbett and Wilfrid Brambell

a personal collection of vintage video-recording machines and he managed to get a picture from the tape which proved that it did indeed feature an episode of *Steptoe and Son*. I handed that tape over to Steve Bryant at the NFTVA and a team of engineers working under Brian Jenkinson started the laborious process of reclaiming the material from the tape. This was no easy task, as the tape and recording system was fairly primitive and age had not helped the condition of the half-inch tape. Painstakingly, however, they persevered and with the eventual success of this first venture, the other tapes were retrieved from Ray Galton.

Later *Steptoe and Son* aficionados Neil Ingoe and Lisa Sargeant (ex president of the Steptoe Society) went along to video an interview with Ray about the find. During the interview Neil and Lisa asked if they could film in the basement where Ray had kept his tapes for so many years. Whilst talking them through the history of the tapes Ray remarked he kept them in a box and indicated a similar box nearby. Upon checking, to the surprise of them all, the box contained more of Ray's tapes. In fact they contained all the rest of the missing episodes bar one ('Men of Property'). Sure, like the others, these were b/w recordings, sometimes of dubious quality, but they were a record of some wonderful moments from a truly classic series.

After one of the MBW events, Neil Ingoe remarked to Brian Jenkinson that most of the tapes had featured two episodes – perhaps they should check the very first tape returned to see if that too had a second episode. Sure enough it was looked at, and marvellously it contained the final missing episode.

Eventually all the episodes were re-recorded onto usable tapes and the BBC screened them in a series they called *The Lost Steptoes*. This was an unprecedented move as they fell short of what could be described 'broadcast quality' but were deemed to be of such cultural importance as to warrant screening. Subsequently they have been released on video.

This is living proof of how material can survive and demonstrates what can be done with some of the most unlikely source material.

CASE STUDY 4: *THE TURN OF THE SCREW*

Director Peter Morley saw Benjamin Britten's opera based on James' ghost story *The Turn of the Screw* and immediately thought it would translate well to TV. He put the idea to his superiors at ATV, suggesting that the opera be performed uncut and be shown without ad breaks. His boss realised the show would have limited audience appeal, but had faith in Morley who had recently been responsible for one of the company's most prestigious (and successful) productions *Tyranny* (see *Tyranny* in 'On the Missing List'). Thus, he agreed to his requests. Benjamin Britten was brought in to oversee the production and the show was scheduled to go out in two 1-hour chunks on consecutive nights (with no ad breaks as Morley had said). Publishing company Boosey and Hawkes owned the copyright to Britten's music and they were worried about reclaiming rights in future on the TV version. They insisted that the opera be wiped a year after its first transmission. Morley needed two studios for the production (one for the dancers – one

The Turn of the Screw

for the orchestra) and so taped the show (as live) at the weekend when ATV – a weekday only broadcaster – had the studios free.

The Turn of the Screw went out with glowing reviews and the predictable negligible audience figures (a TAM rating of zero), although in-depth research revealed that it was actually watched by an audience that could have filled every performance at Sadlers Wells for seven weeks. A private screening of the production was set up, but because the ATV videotape players were in constant use an arrangement was made where a 16mm telerecording would be made after broadcasting hours when the machines were free. However the first attempt was deemed of inferior quality (poor sound, impaired picture quality) so it was junked and a second (acceptable) copy was made. One year after the broadcast, as requested in their contract with Boosey and Hawkes, ATV wiped the tape version and destroyed the 16mm telerecording. That should have been that.

In the 1990s, Peter Morley gave a lecture at the NFT where he mentioned major productions on which he'd worked which no longer existed. He spoke especially about the *The Turn of the Screw*. NFTVA Keeper of Television Steve Bryant circulated a list of these missing items to his staff and one, Fiona O'Brian, connected the missing *The Turn of the Screw* with an unknown 16mm telerecording which the archive had filed under 'miscellaneous'. The recording was checked and proved to be the missing opera. It transpired that this was the inferior first 16mm recording which should have been junked but somehow survived. Despite the poor quality this discovery is a valuable recording of a production of keen interest not only to TV historians, but also to enthusiasts of opera in general and Britten in particular.

PART TWO

ON THE MISSING LIST

On The Missing List

The following section looks in detail at some of the most important missing items from the British archives. The aim here is to alert people (collectors, archivists, industry personnel) as to what's missing in the hope that they may have (or know the whereabouts of) some of the material. There is a distinct possibility that those that may possess such items are not actually aware that they are officially missing. Experience shows that some articles survive minus opening and closing credits and to that end other information (cast, featured artists, storylines, programme descriptions) are included as an aid to identification. The information in this section has been compiled from many different sources, details of which are to be found in the Reference section.

Key

tx: transmitted

ABC: Associated British Picture Corporation – the supplier serving ITV Midlands at the weekends (18.2.56–28.7.68) and ITV North weekends (5.5.56–28.7.68)

A-R: Associated-Rediffusion (just Rediffusion from 1964) – serving London weekdays (22.9.55–29.7.68)

ATV: Associated TeleVision – serving Midlands weekdays (17.2.56–31.12.81, London weekends (24.9.55–28.7.68) and Midlands weekends (2.8.68–30.12.81)

BBC: British Broadcasting Corporation – serving London (1936–9) and building to a national service from 1946

LWT: London Weekend Television – serving London weekends (from 2.8.68)

Timings refer to actual length of material (i.e. an ITV one-hour slot is approximately 50 mins) ITV dates are (predominantly) for the London area transmissions.

COMEDY

DAD'S ARMY

The exploits of the Walmington-on-Sea Home Guard have delighted generations of audiences. Continual repeats and video releases have kept Captain Mainwaring and his motley platoon a well-loved UK TV institution. However, remarkably, five programmes are absent from the series archives.

In his introduction to the book *Dad's Army: The Lost Episodes** (which features the scripts of the missing shows) producer and co-writer David Croft suggests the loss of these programmes may come down to the fact that he was on holiday when permission to wipe the shows was requested. Normally he withheld his permission in such cases, thus most of the 400 plus programmes he was associated with survive in the archives. In his absence on that one occasion somebody else must have given their assent.

Of course it could have been far worse – we might only have five episodes left and had all the others wiped. Great efforts have been made to recover these lost gems – but (so far at least) to no avail.

STOP PRESS – Two episodes recovered as a result of the BBC's Treasure Hunt initiative – see list.

BBC 30 mins, b/w
Series 2
Produced by David Croft
Directed by Harold Snoad
Written by Jimmy Perry and David Croft

Main cast:
Capt George Mainwaring . . . . .Arthur Lowe
Sgt Arthur Wilson . . . . .John Le Mesurier
L-Cpl Jack Jones . . . . .Clive Dunn
Pvt James Frazer . . . . .John Laurie
Pvt Joe Walker . . . . .James Beck
Pvt Charles Godfrey . . . . .Arnold Ridley
Pvt Frank Pike . . . . .Ian Lavender
Pvt Sponge . . . . .Colin Bean

---

* The book *Dad's Army: The Lost Episodes* features the scripts of six episodes but happily one (*Sgt Wilson's Little Secret* – 22.3.69) has survived in the BBC archives.

Operation Kilt (1.3.69)

Guest cast:
Mrs Mavis Pike ....Janet Davies
Capt Ogilvie ....James Copeland

Capt Ogilvie and his crack Highland Regiment arrive to engage the platoon in night time manoeuvres. Their aim is to take Mainwaring's headquarters but they have reckoned without Sgt Wilson's Trojan Horse, and Walker and Frazer's Pantomime Cow.

The Battle of Godfrey's Cottage (8.3.69)

Guest cast:
Mrs Mavis Pike ....Janet Davies
Dolly ....Amy Dalby
Cissy ....Nan Braunton
ARP Warden William Hodges ....Bill Pertwee

When the church bells sound out the signal that the German invasion has started, half the platoon are on a coach bound for the pictures. The others react manfully and hurry to the two pre-arranged spots where they will face the enemy: The Novelty Rock Emporium; and Pvt Godfrey's, cottage where he lives with his two ancient sisters and a rather rude parrot.

The Loneliness of the Long Distance Walker (15.3.69)

Guest cast:
First Brigadier ....Anthony Sharp
Second Brigadier ....Patrick Waddington
Chairwoman ....Diana King
Mr Reed ....Edward Evans
Capt Cutts ....Michael Knowles
Blonde ....Gilda Perry
Soldier ....Larry Martyn
Medical Officer ....Robert Lankesheer

Walker is called up for the regular army much to the distress of the platoon to whom he is valuable as a supplier of black-market items like alcohol and cigarettes. They strive to keep him out of the call-up but to no avail. On his first day in the real army, Walker discovers he is allergic to corned beef. The predominance of the item in the army menu leads to him being honourably discharged and returning to Walmington-on-Sea.

Dad's Army: 'The Loneliness of the Long Distance Walker'

A Stripe for Frazer (29.3.69)

Guest cast:
Captain-Colonel Square . . . . .Geoffrey Lumsden
Capt Bailey . . . . .John Ringham
Policeman .Gordon Peters
Verger . . . . .Edward Sinclair

Capt Mainwaring is allowed to promote from within the service to get a new NCO. He chooses
Frazer as the man, mainly because of his previous record with the navy. Frazer, however, lost his
stripes then when he hit an officer with a boat hook. When he is promoted the power goes to
Frazer's head and he becomes a strict disciplinarian, putting half the platoon on charges.

Under Fire (5.4.69)

Guest cast:
Captain-Colonel Square . . . . .Geoffrey Lumsden
Mrs Mavis Pike . . . . .Janet Davies
Capt Bailey . . . . .John Ringham
ARP Warden William Hodges . . . . . . .Bill Pertwee
Mrs Keen . . . . .Queenie Watts
Mrs Witt . . . . .Gladys Dawson
Sigmund Murphy . . . . .Ernst Ulman

With Britain under heavy fire from the Germans, the platoon have action at last: fire-spotting,
dousing unexploded bombs and putting out fires. They apprehend the Austrian-born Sigmund
Murphy, now a naturalised Britain, whom they suspect of being a Nazi spy. When the church hall
is under fire the platoon react in a chaotic fashion reminiscent of a Keystone Cops comedy. At
the height of their incompetent shenanigans they discover that Murphy, rather than being a spy,
is British through and through. This was the last episode made in b/w.

America had Lucille Ball and Jackie Gleason. Britain had Tony Hancock. A giant figure in the world of both radio and TV comedy in the 1950s, Hancock's depiction of a sometimes boorish, sometimes naive buffoon delighted the nation. The radio shows were hugely popular, but when the visual dimension was added Hancock went on to enjoy even greater success. The early series were performed live and the chances are that there were no recordings made – not officially anyway. One would think that if a home recording (visual and audio) had been made of any of these missing shows, it would have surfaced by now. But strange things happen (like the recent discovery of 35mm colour recordings of pre-war TV – see *Missing, Believed Wiped – Event History* chapter). The recovery of a lost *Hancock's Half-Hour* would be a major find and to that end, here is a brief list of episodes not in the archive.

BBC, 30 mins, b/w
Produced by Duncan Wood
Written by Ray Galton and Alan Simpson

Main Cast
Tony Hancock
Sid James (all but 'Lady Chatterley's Revenge')

SERIES I

The First TV Show (6.7.56)

Guest cast:
Husband . . . . .Harold Goodwin
Wife . . . . .Margaret Flint
Nurse . . . . .Irene Handl
Announcer . . . . .Peter Haigh

Hancock's broken leg jeopardises his first TV show but Sid insists he carries on – even if he has to perform from his hospital bed.

The Artist (20.7.56)

Guest cast:
Art expert . . . . .Valentine Dyall
Model . . . . .Irene Handl
Art dealer . . . . .Warren Mitchell

Hancock fancies himself as an artist and buys some old canvases to paint over. However one of them is a stolen Rembrandt. Determined to get it back the thieves arrange to buy all of Hancock's creations.

___

The Dancer (3.8.56)

Guest cast:
Film producer ....Warren Mitchell
Dance instructor ....Hermione Baddeley
Secretary ....Lorrae Desmond

Hancock has to learn to dance to win a part in a film.

___

The Bequest (17.8.56)

Guest cast:
Mr Witherspoon ....Reginald Beckwith
Miss Medworthy ....Irene Handl
Mrs Batteleaxe ....Rose Howlett
Aunt ....Totti Truman-Taylor
Uncle ....Claude Bonser

In order to receive an inheritance from his uncle, Hancock has to get married. With Sid's help he seeks a wife.

___

The Radio Show (31.8.56)

Guest cast:
Head of TV Variety ....Warren Mitchell
Army Private ....Eric Sykes
Lance Corporal ....Ray Galton
Corporal ....Alan Simpson
Scottish Private ....Ian MacNaughton
Guardsman ....Johnny Vyvyan
Welsh Sergeant ....Graham Stark
With Spike Milligan.

A collection of sketches performed from the 1956 National Radio Show at Earls Court.

The Chef That Died Of Shame (14.9.56)

Guest cast:
Man from the opera . . . . .Warren Mitchell
Martine Dubois . . . . .Constance Wake
Announcer .Peter Haigh
Head Chef .Raymond Rollett

A pie stall cook rises to the dizzy heights of haute cuisine but, alas, falls equally fast due to the demon drink.

SERIES 2

Lady Chatterley's Revenge (14.4.57)

Guest cast:
Lew Silver . . . . .Warren Mitchell
Humphrey Clanger . . . . .John Vere
Producer . . . . .Kenneth Williams
Actress . . . . .Hattie Jacques
Call boy . . . . .Johnny Vyvyan

Hancock has a role in the East Cheam Rep Company's production of *Moon Over Tahiti*, but he is not informed when the play is changed at the eleventh hour to *Lady Chatterley's Revenge*.

The Russian Prince (29.4.57)

Guest cast:
Prince Nicolai . . . . .Kenneth Williams
Countess Olga . . . . .Hattie Jacques
Fred . . . . .Bill Fraser
Prince Paul .Mario Fabrizi
Charlie . . . . .Michael Balfour

A bump on the head causes Hancock to suffer from amnesia. Sid, sensing an opportunity, convinces him he is Prince Nicolai, heir to the fortune of the Russian royal family.

The New Neighbour (13.5.57)

Guest cast:
Secretary ....Hattie Jacques
Policeman ....Kenneth Williams
Clerk ....Bill Fraser
Museum guide ....Mario Fabrizi
Neighbour ....John Vere

Hancock suspects his new neighbour is a murderer disposing of bodies in an incinerator. The truth, however, is that the man works at a wax museum and occasionally has to dispose of the old dummies.

The Pianist (27.5.57)

Guest cast:
Baroness Helen ....Hattie Jacques
Prince Paul ....Kenneth Williams
First aide ....Mario Fabrizi
Second aide ....Roger Oatime
Bird lover ....John Vere

Hancock's imagination runs riot when he gets a job as a nightclub pianist. He dreams of a romance with a wealthy baroness.

The Auction (10.6.57)

Guest cast:
Old man ....Kenneth Williams
Mrs Witherspoon ....Hattie Jacques
Auction attendant ....Manville Tarrant
Croupier ....Mario Fabrizi

Hancock and Sid put all their belongings in an auction in order to raise enough cash to go to Monte Carlo and try out Sid's 'foolproof' roulette system.

SERIES 3

The Continental Holiday (30.9.57)

Guest cast:
Mr X . . . . .Anton Diffring
The Golden Scorpion . . . . .Edouard Assaly
The Black Beetle . . . . .Peter Elliott
The Crimson Alligator . . . . .Alec Bregonzi
The Blue Hedgehog . . . . .Anthony Shirvell
The Green Lizard . . . . .Bruce Wightman
Beggar . . . . .Mario Fabrizi

Hancock returns from a foreign holiday with an unlikely tale of how he foiled a desperate gang
of international smugglers.

The Great Detective (7.10.57)

Guest cast:
Rupert . . . . .John Vere
Patricia . . . . .Peggy Ann Clifford
The Colonel . . . . .Cameron Hall
Colonel's wife . . . . .Evelyn Lund
John . . . . .Terence Alexander
Cynthis . . . . .Totti Truman-Taylor
Matilda . . . . .Pat Coombs
Body . . . . .Johnny Vyvyan

Hancock imagines himself as ace mystery solver Sexton Hancock, investigating a baffling murder plot.

The Amusement Arcade (14.10.57)

Guest cast:
Educated Albert . . . . .Bill Fraser
Councillor Sproggs . . . . .John Vere
Listener . . . . .Alec Bregonzi
Ballot teller . . . . .Dick Emery
Voter . . . . .Johnny Vyvyan

Hancock is up for election to the local council on an anti-sleaze ticket. If he's successful he plans to lead a campaign to shut down Sid's amusement arcade.

A Holiday In Scotland (21.10.57)

Guest cast:
Doctor . . . . .Raymond Huntley
First weatherman . . . . .Ian MacNaughton
Second weatherman . . . . .Richard Statman
Nurse . . . . .Anne Marryott
Mrs Brown .Eileen Delamare

The doctor is worried about the state of Hancock's health – the result is Hancock and Sid travelling to Scotland on a hunting holiday to get fit.

The Regimental Reunion (4.11.57)

Guest cast:
Mr Spooner .Campbell Singer
Ex-Major . . . . .Terence Alexander
Ex-Colonel . . . . .Graham Leaman
Ex-Captain . . . . .Guy Middleton
Mr Filley . . . . .John Vere
First Millionaire . . . . .George Crowther
Second Millionaire . . . . .Arthur Mullard
Third Millionaire . . . . .Harry Robbins

For nearly twenty years Hancock has laboured as an office junior in a city firm. At a regimental reunion he meets up with his old army colleagues and they place large orders with Hancock's company, earning him a promotion. However, the whiff of fraud is everywhere.

The Adopted Family (11.11.57)

Guest cast:
Secretary . . . . .Anne Marryott
Housing Officer . . . . .Ian Fleming

Judge . . . . .John Vere
Young wife .Anne Reid
Young husband . . . . .Stuart Hillier
First son . . . . .Hugh Lloyd
Second son . . . . .Mario Fabrizi
Third son .Johnny Vyvyan
Fourth son . . . . .Manville Tarrant

Hancock tries to con himself into a council flat by finding a wife and adopting four sons (actually all friends of Sid). But once he has his family he finds it hard to get rid of them.

The Elocution Teacher (25.11.57)

Guest cast:
As himself .Jack Hawkins
Ponsonby Everest . . . . .John Vere
Mrs Fazkerly . . . . .Nora Nicholson
Miss Perkins . . . . .Mary Reynolds
Announcer .Stuart Hillier

When famous actor Jack Hawkins puts himself under Hancock's tutelage for elocution lessons he gets more than he bargained for: eventually his diction is so bad he can only get a job as a rock'n'roll singer.

SERIES 4

Underpaid! Or Grandad's SOS (26.12.58)

Guest cast:
Frederick Higgins . . . . .George Crowther
Sharebuyer . . . . .Arthur Mullard
Australian barman . . . . .Rolf Harris
Phyllis . . . . .Evelyn Lund
Arthur Biggs . . . . .Harry Drew

On hearing that Hancock's millionaire grandfather is on his death bed, Sid travels to Australia masquerading as Hancock to get his hands on what he hopes will be a sizeable inheritance.

The Flight of the Red Shadow (23.1.59)

Guest cast:
Arab . . . . .Mario Fabrizi
Barracker . . . . .Ray Galton
Warder . . . . .Alan Simpson
Manager . . . . .Robert Dorning
Balloon seller . . . . .Alec Bregonzi
Sailor . . . . .Rolf Harris
Policeman .Arthur Mullard
Vicar . . . . .John Vere

When *The Desert Song* closes the cast are after impresario and lead actor Sid and Hancock for their wages. They flee, dressed in their stage costumes, but Hancock is mistaken for a visiting Maharajah and has to make a speech.

The Horror Serial (30.1.59)

Guest cast:
Colonel . . . . .John Le Mesurier
Lieutenant .Dennis Chinnery
First soldier . . . . .Alec Bregonzi
Second soldier . . . . .Johnny Vyvyan
Third soldier . . . . .Laurie Webb
Sergeant . . . . .Hugh Lloyd
Mr Biggs . . . . .Arthur Mullard
Mrs Biggs .Phyllis Norwood
Nurse . . . . .Anne Marryott

The scary last episode of horror serial *Quatermass and the Pit* has left Hancock a nervous wreck. When he finds a strange object buried in his garden Hancock is convinced it's a Martian space craft – but Sid thinks it's an unexploded World War II bomb and calls in the army.

The Italian Maid (6.2.59)

Guest cast:
Italian maid . . . . .Marla Landi
Domestic agent . . . . .John Vere

Italian father . . . . .Harry Lane
Italian mother . . . . .Betty Lloyd-Davies
Swiss man .Frederick Schiller
Telegram boy . . . . .Johnny Vyvyan

When Hancock's new maid turns out to be a dusky beauty both Sid and Hancock try and woo her. Hancock ends up doing most of the housework for her, he is so enamoured. Things turn from bad to worse when her entire family turn up for a visit.

Matrimony – Almost (13.2.59)

Guest cast:
Reggie . . . . .Terence Alexander
Percy . . . . .Cardew Robinson
Mr Wetherby . . . . .Cameron Hall
Elizabeth .Vivienne Martin
Vicar . . . . .John Vere
Freddie . . . . .Mario Fabrizi
First broker's man . . . . .Ivor Raymonde
Second broker's man . . . . .Arthur Mullard

Hancock meets a girl at Sid's pyjama party for the wealthy upper classes. Sid tells Hancock the girl is rich and says the same thing to the girl about Hancock. With thoughts of the other's riches in their minds the pair hastily arrange to get married..

The Beauty Contest (20.2.59)

Guest cast:
The Mayor .John Vere
Alderman Biggs . . . . .Robert Dorning
Alderman Jones . . . . .James Bulloch
Gym instructor . . . . .Roger Avon
Jim Banstead . . . . .Johnny Vyvyan
Percy Whyteleaf . . . . .Mario Fabrizi
Arnold Nonsuch . . . . .Arthur Mullard
Henry Mortlake . . . . .George Crowther

The East Cheam council decide not to hold a traditional beauty contest due to the poor quality of the entrants. Instead they opt for a Mr East Cheam competition. Both Hancock and Sid enter, equally convinced that they will win.

The Wrong Man (6.3.59)

Guest cast:
Constable . . . . .Roger Avon
Sergeant . . . . .James Bulloch
Inspector . . . . .Campbell Singer
Detective Soames . . . . .Harry Locke
Cinema cashier . . . . .Pamela Manson
Bruiser . . . . .Arthur Mullard
Little man .Johnny Vyvyan

Hancock is asked to take part in an identity parade to make up the numbers but is picked out by three eye witnesses as the robber. Protesting his innocence Hancock sets out to find the real culprit.

The Servants (27.3.59)

Guest cast:
Colonel Winthrop . . . . .John Le Mesurier
Mrs Winthrop . . . . .Mary Hinton
Secretary .Alec Bregonzi
First old man . . . . .Hugh Lloyd
Second old man . . . . .Charles Julian
Third old man . . . . .Gordon Phillott
First old woman . . . . .Nancy Roberts
Second old woman . . . . .Evelyn Lund
Third old woman . . . . .Patricia Hayes

With the TV series over, Hancock and Sid find themselves in need of jobs. Masquerading as an elderly couple they take up employment as servants to the Winthrops – however, suspicions are raised when the pair start taking turns at being the woman.

THE LIKELY LADS

Steptoe and Son proved to the BBC that sitcoms could benefit immeasurably by the booking of established actors to play the leads rather than comedy stars which had been the usual policy following the success of *Hancock's Half-Hour*, *Sykes* and *The Dickie Henderson Show*. With *The Likely Lads* they struck gold again with the inspired pairing of James Bolam and Rodney Bewes. The two excelled in the raunchy, risqué scripts from Dick Clement and Ian La Frenais which charted the frustrations and triumphs of two working-class blokes living in the north-east of England. Launched on the newly created, second BBC channel, BBC2, the show quickly became one of the channel's early successes, although with a limited viewing audience. When the shows were repeated on BBC1 they were finally able to get the huge audiences the sharp writing and fine acting deserved. The series returned in the 1970s as *Whatever Happened to the Likely Lads*, arguably a better and more rounded piece of work than the original series, but it would be useful now if we could have even more of the original to make that sort of comparison. In 1999 a missing episode ('Last of the Big Spenders' 7.7.65) was unearthed (see full story in 'Missing Believed Wiped – Event History' chapter), so there is a chance that other 16mm telerecordings may have survived. These are the missing episodes:

BBC, 30 mins b/w

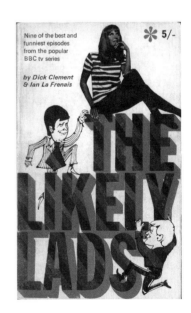

Main cast:
Terry Collier . . . . .James Bolam
Bob Ferris .Rodney Bewes

Other regulars:
Audrey Collier . . . . .Sheila Fearn
Jack . . . . .Don McKillop
Blakey . . . . .Richard Moore
Cloughy . . . . .Bartlett Mullins
Mrs Ferris .Irene Richmond
Mrs Collier .Olive Milbourne

Written by: Dick Clement and Ian La Frenais
Produced by: Dick Clement

Chance of a Lifetime (13.1.65)

Guest cast:
Cecile   . . . . .Veronica Lang
Wally Ralph   . . . . .Barry Linehan
Jeffcock   . . . . .Garfield Morgan
Barman   . . . . .Eric Smith

Fed up after being rained on and stood up by two lasses, the lads take refuge in the station hotel where they meet a chap who regales them with stories of the delights of Adelaide. In their present mood, escape to Australia sounds like just what the doctor ordered and they contemplate emigration. The man offers to help them get the £10 assisted passage providing they get the money to him pretty sharpish. But getting the money isn't as easy as it sounds …

Baby It's Cold Outside (16.6.65)

Guest cast:
Margaret . . . . .Dorothy White
Rose . . . . .Kate Storey
June . . . . .Janet Kelly
Barman . . . . .John Scott Martin

The lads are double dating and need somewhere to take the girls. They offer to babysit for a friend and take the girls back to his place whilst convincing them that it's actually their pad. All goes well until the baby awakes and starts crying …

A Star is Born (23.6.65)

Guest cast:
Rhona . . . . .Dilys Watling
Freddy Fyfe .Bernard Spear

When Jack gets up and sings at his birthday party the lads take the mick out of him. But beautiful waitress singer Rhona castigates them and challenges them to do better at the talent contest taking place the next Saturday. Despite their lack or musical talent the boys are sorely tempted, Bob with his eye on the £25 prize money, Terry with his eye on Rhona …

The Talk of the Town (30.6.65)

Guest cast:
Helen . . . . .Helen Fraser
Big Duggie . . . . .Michael Coles

After a wild party Bob wakes up with a hangover and a hazy memory of the previous night. He is puzzled when friends keep congratulating him and then shocked when he is told he got engaged to a girl called Helen the previous night. Bob can remember walking Helen home, but little else. When the rumour goes round that she's pregnant, Bob steels himself to face the music …

Far Away Places (14.7.65)

Guest cast:
Archie . . . . .Norman Chappell
Eva . . . . .Gay Hamilton
Labour Exchange clerk . . . . .Roger Avon

Taking girls out has depleted the lads' cash reserves, a desperate situation with the holidays looming. So grave is their plight that they even look into the possibility of getting some part-time work to bring in a little extra …

Where Have all the Flowers Gone? (21.7.65)

Guest Cast:
Marlo . . . . .George Leyton
Beryl . . . . .Janina Faye
Elaine . . . . .Tracy Rogers

At a family wedding the lads are being quizzed about when they will settle down and get married. It seems all their friends have gone down the aisle and they are the last of a dying breed. Are they too old for the single life?

The Likely Lads: 'Outward Bound'

SERIES 3

Outward Bound (4.6.66)

Guest cast:
Café owner . . . . .Keith Roberts
Scoutmaster .James Cossins
Postmistress .Amy Dalby
Valerie . . . . .Nerys Hughes
Susan . . . . .Sandra Blaine

The lads are lured to a coastal resort where rumour has it Beatniks hang out and indulge in 'free love'. But the trip goes seriously awry and the boys find themselves stranded, cold and tired when the last train has gone and their overnight stop has been demolished to make way for a housing estate.

Friends and Neighbours (11.6.66)

Guest cast:
Grandad . . . . .Wilfred Lawson
Mr Perrin . . . . .Glen Melvyn
Mrs Perrin .Noël Dyson
Lorna Perrin . . . . .Angela Lovell
Barmaid . . . . .Rita Ramano

Terry's grandad is staying at Terry's aunt's house while she is away in Canada. However Grandad's rather uncouth manner upsets the neighbours Mr and Mrs Perrin. To make matters worse, Bob is dating the Perrins' daughter Lorna and he sides with the Perrins against Terry and his Grandad.

Brief Encounter (25.6.66)

Guest cast:
Ursula . . . . .Isobel Black
Jack . . . . .Donald McKillop
Drunk . . . . .Donald Oliver
Waitress . . . . .Maggie Riley
Girl . . . . .Joan Pickering
Barman . . . . .Lewis Teasdale

At a local dance the boys split up to improve their chances of scoring, but ultimately set their sights on the same girl, the bewitching Ursula.

The Razor's Edge (2.7.66)

Guest cast:
Darby . . . . .Antony Baird
Godfrey . . . . .Donald Gee
Monica . . . . .Vickery Turner
Podge . . . . .Geoffrey Hughes
Barmaid . . . . .Penelope Goddard
Barman . . . . .John Scott Martin

Whilst in incubation due to his chicken pox, Bob grows a beard. Terry mocks his hairy friend, but Bob likes the look and intends on keeping the growth. However, Mr Darby, their boss at work, dislikes his new look and orders him to shave his beard off. Terry sees this as victimisation and prepares to fight Bob's corner, even if it does mean Bob may lose his job.

Anchors Aweigh (9.7.66)

Guest cast:
Sam . . . . .Hamish Roughead
Sally West . . . . .Rosemary Nicols
Barman . . . . .Patrick Carter
Marion . . . . .Glenda Ramsay

On a boating holiday on the Norfolk Broads an otherwise idyllic time is marred when the boys fall out over a couple of girls.

Love and Marriage (16.7.66)

Guest cast:
Helen . . . . .Helen Fraser
Duggie . . . . .Derek Newark
Archie . . . . .Norman Chappell
Mrs Foster . . . . .Elizabeth Begley
Podge . . . . .Geoffrey Hughes
Old Dan . . . . .Frank Cowley

The lads are preparing for a friend's stag night at the local social club. Whilst waiting for Norman, the groom-to-be, they meet up with Duggie, an old friend now married with a child, who has popped in for a quick one on the way home. They persuade him to stay and help him get well and truly sozzled. When Norman fails to show, the lads realise they have got the wrong night, but all is not wasted as they have learnt some valuable things about the state of being married and the allure of staying single.

NOT ONLY ... BUT ALSO

Originally conceived as a showcase for Dudley Moore, with Peter Cook in a subsidiary role, *Not Only ... But Also* introduced a partnership that was to prove hugely popular. Cook, the brilliant satirist, found the perfect foil in the diminutive Dagenham boy Dud and their double-act resulted in some of the funniest moments ever seen on the small screen. Thankfully much material from the series survives, but sadly a considerable amount doesn't. In the early 1990s the BBC replayed most of the surviving segments in a series they called *The Best of ... What's Left Of ... Not Only ... But Also*. A video release followed shortly after. Here's the lowdown on what was not left.

BBC, 30 mins b/w
Produced by: Joe McGrath (Series 1), Dick Clement (Series 2), James Gilbert (Series 3)

Not Only ... – Dudley Moore – *But Also ...* – Peter Cook

SERIES 1 – actually entitled *Not Only … But Also …* (Editions 1–4 survive)
7 x 45 mins, b/w

Edition 5 (6.3.65)

Guest . . . . .Mel Torme

Sketches include: The Employee; Pete and Dud – On the Bus. (Film sequences *do exist* for 'Cigarette Adveriting'; 'Political Canvassing in Transylvania')

Edition 6 (20.3.65)

Guests . . . . .Peter Sellers, T-Bone Walker

Sketches include: The Gourmet; Boxer-cum-artist; Pete and Dud – Superstition

Edition 7 (3.4.65)

Guests . . . . .Eric Sykes, Blossom Dearie

Sketches include: Film Studio; Pete and Dud – Religions

SERIES 2 – (Editions 1 and 7 survive)
7 x 30 mins, b/w

Edition 2 (22.1.66)

Guests . . . . .Alan Freeman, Katie Boyle, Percy Thrower, Jacqui Chan

Sketches include: Six of the Best; Most Boring Man in the World; Pete and Dud – Disease

Edition 3 (29.1.66)

Guest . . . . .Emily Yancy

Sketches include: Italian Restaurant; Blue Movie. (A sketch from this edition, 'Ol' Man River', has survived on 16mm)

Edition 4 (5.2.66)

Guest . . . . .Blossom Dearie

Sketches include: Commercials; The Frog and Peach

Edition 5 (12.2.66)

Guest . . . . .Dionne Warwick

Sketches include: Psychiatrist; The Epic that Never Was; Father and Son

Edition 6 (19.2.66)

Guest . . . . .Dusty Springfield

Sketches include: Pete and Dud – Sex (Film sequences *do exist* for: 'Walrus and the Carpenter'; 'Drinking Song')

SERIES 3
7 x 30 mins, colour

Edition 1 (18.2.70)

Guest . . . . .Spike Milligan

Sketches include: The Piano Tuner; Pete and Dud – Dreams. (A sketch from this edition, 'Bargo', has survived on 16mm)

Edition 2 (4.3.70)

Guests . . . . .Willie Rushton, Joe Cocker

Sketches include: Tits and Bums; Pete and Dud – Double-O Dud (A sketch from this edition, 'The Glidd of Glood', has survived on 16mm)

Edition 3 (18.3.70)

Guest . . . . .Barry Humphries

Sketches include: Sir Arthur Greeb-Streebling's World of Worms; Train Conductor; In The Club; Pete and Dud – Racial Prejudice

Edition 4 (1.4.70)

Guests . . . . .Frank Muir, Alan Price

Sketches include: Good vs Evil Cricket Match; Permission to Marry; Psycho; Pete and Dud – The Futility of Life

Edition 5 (15.4.70)

Guest . . . . .Ronnie Barker

Sketches include: Sir Arthur Greeb-Streebling: Flowers; Permission to Wed; Undercover Doctor; Pete and Dud – Writing A Bestseller. (A sketch from this edition, 'This is Ludwig Van Beethoven', has survived on 16mm)

Edition 6 (29.4.70)

Guest . . . . .Denis Norden

Sketches include: Newspaper; Lengths; Pete and Dud – As Nature Intended

Edition 7 (13.5.70)

Guests . . . . .Alan Bennett, John Williams

Sketches include: Jumbo and Teddy; Pete and Dud – The Artist (Two sketches from this edition: 'Cyclist on the Ark Royal' and 'The Making of A Movie' survive on 16mm)

ON THE MARGIN

Alan Bennett's series of comedy sketches, monologues, poems and songs has long been considered one of the greatest losses from the archives. *On The Margin* featured in embryo all of the telling observation and bittersweet irony that would distinguish Bennett's later work. It was warmly received at the time and the BBC repeated the series twice (once on its originating channel, BBC2, and later to a wider audience on BBC1) within six months. Many years after its loss, Alan Bennett talked about the junking of the show and reprised one of the series skits on Channel 4's 1990 New Year's Day special *The A to Z of Television*. Audio recordings of the series exist and a commercially available album of highlights was issued.

BBC 9.11.66–14.12.66
6 x 30 mins, b/w

Produced by: Patrick Garland
Directed by: Sydney Lotterby
Written by: Alan Bennett

Cast:
Alan Bennett
John Sergeant
Roland MacLeod
Madge Hindle
Virginia Stride
Yvonne Gilan

Comedy poems, sketches and songs featured every week as did archive clips of famous music hall acts. A recurring sketch 'Streets Ahead' eavesdropped on 'the life and times in NW1' and featured two couples the Knocker-Threws (Nigel and Jane) and the Touch-Paceys.

A film item from a sketch entitled 'Norwich' from the second edition (16.11.66) has survived.

On the Margin: Alan Bennett

Johnny Speight's acerbic comedy driven by the arguments between two conflicting generations in one working-class family revolutionised the sitcom on both sides of the Atlantic (the US series *All in the Family*, based on the format of *Till Death Us Do Part*, proving equally groundbreaking when it debuted in the US in 1971). Speight created a monster in the bigoted, right-wing Alf Garnett – a character made flesh by the consistently wonderful performance by Warren Mitchell. Indeed Mitchell's portrayal was so well rounded that it's possible he imbued Garnett with a humanity beyond his depiction in the scripts, inadvertently adding to the controversy that has always dogged the series. There has never been any doubt about Speight's motives – he set out to ridicule the xenophobic, jingoistic, philosophy of Alf Garnett and his like – but the very act of airing such views in a television comedy programme itself raised concerns. Some viewers actually agreed with Alf and missed the whole point of the show.

Arguments have long surrounded the series but few would contest its quality as a sharply written, important piece of comedy. The surviving episodes from the series have often been repeated (even, scandalously, in a bowdlerised form) but the great majority of the landmark 1960s episodes have been lost. The scripts for these episodes indicate that they were from the show's golden period, harsher and more shocking than the later 70s series.

STOP PRESS – Two episodes subsequently recovered.

Comedy Playhouse: 'Till Death Us Do Part'
BBC tx 22.7.65, 30 mins b/w

Cast:
Alf Ramsey . . . . .Warren Mitchell
Elsie Ramsey . . . . .Gretchen Franklin
Rita . . . . .Una Stubbs
Mike . . . . .Anthony Booth

We meet the Ramseys, an East End family who constantly argue. An extract exists.

Till Death Us Do Part
BBC, b/w
Writer: Johnny Speight
Producer: Dennis Main Wilson

Cast:
Alf Garnett . . . . .Warren Mitchell
Else Garnett   . . . . .Dandy Nichols
Rita . . . . .Una Stubbs
Mike . . . . .Anthony Booth

SERIES 1

Arguments, Arguments … (6.6.66) – extract exists

Guest cast: Will Stampe, Rita Webb, Charlie Bird, Fred McNaughton, Paul Lindley.

Reworking of Comedy Playhouse script with the family name now established as Garnett.

Hair Raising! (13.6.66)

Guest cast: Will Stampe, Charlie Bird, Henry Longhurst, Wally Patch, Fred McNaughton, Paul Lindley, Eddie Malin

Alf tries putting paraffin on his head to promote hair growth, but to no avail. When Alf falls into a deep sleep in the chair Mike can't help using Rita's lipstick to draw a face on Alf's head. Mike goes to get Rita to come down and look but when they get down there Alf has gone to the pub.

Intolerance (27.6.66) – extract exists

Guest cast: Thomas Baptiste, Will Stampe, Frank Gatliffe, Pat Coombs, Dennis Golding, Pamela Oswald, Theodore Wilhelm, John Young, Peter Kelly.

Special guests: Ian St John, Willie Stevenson.

Two Toilets? … That's Posh (4.7.66)

Guest cast: Arnold Diamond

Mike and Rita decide the house is too small and try and convince Alf that they all need to move to a larger place.

From Liverpool With Love (18.7.66)

Guest cast: Patrick McAlinney, Julia Jones, Will Stampe, Charlie Bird, Fred McNaughton

Mike's mother and father are paying a visit. Reluctantly Alf welcomes them into his home but he finds Mike's dad even worse than his randy scouse git of a son.

Claustrophobia (1.8.66)

Guest cast: Sydney Bromley, Kenneth Fortescue, Victor Platt, Jerold Wells, Felicity Brown.

The pressure of sharing a small, cramped Cornwall holiday cottage proves almost too much for the arguing Garnetts.

SERIES 2

Sex Before Marriage (2.1.67) – extract exists

Guest cast: John Junkin, Leslie Noyes.

Whilst decorating the house the conversation somehow gets round to investigating whether Mike and Rita had had sex before they got married.

I Can Give It Up Anytime I Like (9.1.67)

Mike has a bad cough and Rita is on at him to give up smoking for a while. Alf insists that pipe smoking is a lot healthier than smoking fags. After a heated argument the pair bet on who can give up for the longest. The girls are referees, with the incentive that whoever catches one of the men smoking will win all the money they'd normally spend on tobacco (which is being squirrelled away in a jar).

The Bulldog Breed (16.1.67)

Guest cast: Roy Kinnear, Fred McNaughton

Mike and Alf are arguing about the Vietnam War when a man parks a van outside Alf's house blocking the light coming in through the window. An enraged Alf goes out to remonstrate with the driver (Roy Kinnear) but comes back shaking with fear.

Caviare on the Dole (23.1.67)

Guest cast: Dermot Kelly, Robert Dorning, Will Stampe, Barbara Keogh, Lewis Ward

Mike is made redundant and starts to live in idle luxury – much to Alf's chagrin.

Till Death Us Do Part: 'A Wapping Mythology' – Warren Mitchell and Anthony Booth

A Woman's Place is in the Home! (30.1.67)

Guest cast: Geraldine Sherman, Fanny Carby, Lewis Ward, Julie May

When Alf returns home late after doing overtime he finds the rest of the family out and his dinner in the oven burnt to a crisp. He rants and raves at them when they come back but agrees to have fish and chips from Wally's fish bar. However, getting his dinner proves surprisingly difficult.

A Wapping Mythology (The Worker's King) (6.2.67)

Guest cast: Will Stampe

The two generations in the Garnett household are split when Liverpool play West Ham.

In Sickness and in Health … (13.2.67)

Guest cast: Graham Stark, Anthony Sharp, Mark Eden, Tommy Godfrey, Valerie Murray.

Alf is ill and makes everyone feel sick.

State Visit (20.2.67)

The Garnett's discuss the visit to Britain of the Russian premier. Alf and Else decide to visit Downing Street and Buckingham Palace to register in person their protest at the visit.

SERIES 3

The Phone (5.1.68)

Guest cast: Will Stampe, Pat Coombs

Alf's neighbours are taking liberties with Alf's new phone – and his family aren't helping either.

Monopoly (19.1.68)

New Year's Eve and the family are playing Monopoly and discussing various subjects (like 'how come Alf never goes to church despite supporting God' and 'how easy it is to play golf'). Then the rest of the family go to a party next door to which Alf hasn't been invited. Alf intends to watch TV for the evening, but the electricity meter runs out and Alf is all out of shillings.

The Funeral (26.1.68)

Guest cast: Joan Sims, Bill Fraser, Will Stampe, Frank Howard

The funeral of a neighbour, Mrs Weatherby, makes Alf think about his own mortality. Even in death you've got your troubles, Alf decides, when the local cornershop man complains that Mrs Weatherby still owed him two weeks' money, and Gran, confusing the funeral for a wedding, starts a sing-song with Elsie.

Football (2.2.68)

Hammers fan Alf tries to teach the young generation how to play football and keep off the streets.

The Puppy – aka The Dog (9.2.68)

Alf arrives home one Sunday lunchtime with a mongrel puppy he has bought from a guy in the pub. He tries to impress the family with his knowledge of dogs.

Aunt Maud (16.2.68)

Guest cast: Ann Lancaster, Edward Evans

Tension in the house. Mum is ill in bed and Aunt Maud has come from Southend to look after the family. Trouble is Alf and Aunt Maud don't see eye to eye.

Please note, elements of these scripts were reused in later (colour) episodes of *Till Death Us Do Part* and *In Sickness and In Health*. The above missing episodes are all b/w.

DRAMA

ARMCHAIR THEATRE

The ABC Version

In the 1950s the imminent launch of commercial television in Britain worried some people. The BBC would lose their monopoly, now having to compete with a sparky upstart that seemed to have unlimited funds. Many were concerned that we were heading towards the US model of television, a sponsor-led, advertising dominated medium where the programmes seemed mere filler for the selling spots (this showed a lack of understanding of American TV which, at the time, was enjoying a golden era of fine solo dramas and landmark variety shows to offset its more simplistic fare).

In the event, ITV confounded its critics by including, in addition to its US imports and brash variety shows, some outstanding home-grown drama. Plays were a staple of the 1950s schedules and the most famous strand of them all was *Armchair Theatre*, a Sunday night audience magnet which presented top-quality casts in memorable adaptations and original stories. The series began in 1956 but, good as it was even then, it would become even greater in 1958 with the arrival of Canadian producer Sydney Newman. Newman propelled the series in new directions, upping the percentage of scripts especially written for television. This provided work for literally dozens of writers new to the medium, and some would go on to glittering careers. This stellar work continued under the proprietorship of Leonard White, who took over when Newman left to work at the BBC.

ABC produced over 400 editions of the series before the mantle passed to Thames in 1968. Less than a third survive today in the archives. There follows a list of the 125 plays which *have survived*. All other titles are thought to be lost.

SURVIVING EDITIONS

ABC EDITIONS OF ARMCHAIR THEATRE

15.9.57	*Now Let Him Go*
24.11.57	*The Human Touch*
16.2.58	*The Lady of the Camellias*
30.3.58	*The Emperor Jones*
13.4.58	*Wolf Pack*
4.5.58	*Breach of Marriage*
25.5.58	*Death of Satan*
1.6.58	*The Widower*
3.8.58	*The Travelling Lady*

12.10.58 . . . .*I Can Destroy the Sun*
26.10.58 . . . .*The Terrorist*
9.11.58 . . . .*The Greatest Man in the World*
28.12.58 . . . .*The Criminals*
4.1.59 . . . .*The Sentry*
25.1.59 . . . .*Love and Money*
1.2.59 . . . .*Hot Summer Night*
8.3.59 . . . .*The Bird, The Bear and the Actress*
16.8.59 . . . .*You'll Never See Me Again*
13.9.59 . . . .*The Scent of Fear*
20.9.59 . . . .*After the Show*
27.9.59 . . . .*Worm in the Bud*
11.10.59 . . . .*The Thought of Tomorrow*
8.11.59 . . . .*Small Fish are Sweet*
15.11.59 . . . .*The Last of the Brave*
6.12.59 . . . .*Dr Kabil*
10.1.60 . . . .*Where I Live*
3.4.60 . . . .*After the Funeral*
24.4.60 . . . .*A Night Out*

Series ran as Armchair Mystery Theatre 5.6.60–4.9.60

5.6.60 . . . .*Eye Witness*
3.7.60 . . . .*Toff and Fingers*
10.7.60 . . . .*Flight from Treason*
7.8.60 . . . .*False Witness*
4.9.60 . . . .*The Dummy*

25.9.60 . . . .*Lena, O My Lena*
23.10.60 . . . .*I'll Have You to Remember*
30.10.60 . . . .*My Representative*
11.12.60 . . . .*The Cupboard*
29.1.61 . . . .*Honeymoon Postponed*
26.2.61 . . . .*Tune on an Apron String*
5.3.61 . . . .*The Big Deal*
12.3.61 . . . .*The Man Out There*
9.4.61 . . . .*The Ways of Love*
7.5.61 . . . .*Danger, Men Working*
2.7.61 . . . .*The Ship That Couldn't Stop*
10.9.61 . . . .*The Omega Mystery*

8.10.61 . . . .*The Rose Affair*
19.11.61 . . . .*The Trouble With Our Ivy*
17.12.61 . . . .*Tune on an Old Tax Fiddle*
6.5.62 . . . .*Night Conspirators*
8.7.62 . . . .*The Hard Knock*
19.8.62 . . . .*The Fishing Match*
2.9.62 . . . .*Nothing To Pay*
30.9.62 . . . .*Afternoon of a Nymph*
28.10.62 . . . .*Always Something Hot*
25.11.62 . . . .*The Big Ride*
23.12.62 . . . .*Hear the Tiger, See the Bay*
6.1.63 . . . .*Blue and White*
20.1.63 . . . .*The Hot Potato Boys*
3.2.63 . . . .*Into the Dark*
17.2.63 . . . .*The Paradise Suite*
31.3.63 . . . .*The Invasion*
28.4.63 . . . .*Wagger*
9.6.63 . . . .*The Monkey and the Mohawk*
23.6.63 . . . .*The Push-Over*
7.7.63 . . . .*Late Summer*
21.7.63 . . . .*A Little Night Music*
4.8.63 . . . .*The Snag*
18.8.63 . . . .*Living Image*
15.9.63 . . . .*The Front Room*
13.10.63 . . . .*Little Doris*
27.10.63 . . . .*The Chocolate Tree*
17.11.63 . . . .*Long Past Glory*
1.12.63 . . . .*The Higher They Fly*
15.12.63 . . . .*The Swindler*
29.12.63 . . . .*A Way of Living*
12.1.64 . . . .*Sharp at Four*
26.1.64 . . . .*Last Word on Julie*
5.4.64 . . . .*Prisoner and Escort*
26.4.64 . . . .*A Nice Little Business*
3.5.64 . . . .*Pleasure Where She Finds It*
7.6.64 . . . .*That's Where The Town's Going!*

Series ran as Armchair Mystery Theatre 19.7.64–6.9.64

19.7.64 . . . .*Time Out of Mind*
26.7.64 . . . .*The Blackmailing of Mr S*

13.9.64 . . . .*The Trial of Dr Fancy*
27.9.64 . . . .*The Cherry on the Top*
15.1.64 . . . .*The Importance of Being Earnest*
13.12.64 . . . .*The Hothouse*
3.1.65 . . . .*I've Got a System*
14.2.65 . . . .*The Lady with the Albatross*
14.3.65 . . . .*I Took My Little World Away*
18.4.65 . . . .*The Man Who Came to Die*

Series ran as Armchair Mystery Theatre 9.5.65–26.9.65

13.6.65 . . . .*Man and Mirror*
19.9.65 . . . .*Ask Any Neighbour*

4.12.65 . . . .*The Paraffin Season*
11.12.65 . . . .*The Gong Game*
18.12.65 . . . .*A Cold Peace*
15.1.66 . . . .*Neighbours*
22.1.66 . . . .*The Pity of it All*
19.3.66 . . . .*Man Without a Mortgage*
2.4.66 . . . .*The Night Before the Morning After*
9.4.66 . . . .*Don't Utter a Note*
23.4.66 . . . .*The Walls Came Tumbling Down*
30.4.66 . . . .*The Match*
6.8.66 . . . .*The One-Eyed Monster*
3.9.66 . . . .*The Noise Stopped*
10.9.66 . . . .*Dead Silence*
17.9.66 . . . .*Barret Keller – His Mark*
24.9.66 . . . .*Light the Blue Touch Paper*
28.1.67 . . . .*The Floating Population*
4.2.67 . . . .*A Magnum for Schneider*
11.2.67 . . . .*What's Wrong With Humpty Dumpty?*
25.2.67 . . . .*Easier in the Dark*
4.3.67 . . . .*Reason for Sale*
8.4.67 . . . .*Call Me Daddy*
15.4.67 . . . .*I Am Osango*

Series ran as Armchair Thriller 22.4.67-20.5.67

29.4.67 . . . .*England My England*
6.5.67 . . . .*In the Name of the Law*

1.7.67 . . . .*Compensation Alice*
29.7.67 . . . .*Love Life*
5.8.67 . . . .*The Education of Corporal Halliday*
2.9.67 . . . .*Split Level*
9.9.67 . . . .*Poor Cherry*
3.2.68 . . . .*Mr Capper's Birthday*
10.2.68 . . . .*The Wind in a Tall Paper Chimney*
17.2.68 . . . .*The Scallop Shell*
9.3.68 . . . .*A Very Fine Line*

The vast majority of the titles above survive as b/w 16mm telerecordings. This is the most likely format for any future discoveries from the series.

THE THAMES VERSION

ABC's franchise passed to the new company, Thames, in 1968 and the following year Thames launched their version of *Armchair Theatre*. They produced a further 73 plays, of which happily 64 survive.

In this case the following list details the Thames editions which HAVE NOT SURVIVED.

6.1.69 . . . .*The Frobisher Game*
13.1.69 . . . .*A Foot in the Door*
20.1.69 . . . .*What's A Mother For?*
27.1.69 . . . .*The Mandarins*
3.2.69 . . . .*Go On – It'll Do You Good*
10.2.69 . . . .*The Good Son*
17.2.69 . . . .*The Brophy Story*
3.3.69 . . . .*The Story-Teller*
10.3.69 . . . .*On Vacation*

These are all from the first Thames season of plays. The only surviving episode from that period (*Edward the Confessor*) exists as a 16mm b/w telerecording, thus it is likely that this will be the format for any further survivors.

THE AVENGERS

Internationally famous and successful fantasy action series starring Patrick Macnee as secret agent John Steed, assisted on weird and wonderful adventures by numerous colleagues – most memorably his sexy and lethal lady partners Cathy Gale (Honor Blackman) and Emma Peel (Diana Rigg).

When the show debuted however, many of the things that would make it famous just weren't there – no girls, no champagne, no recognisable Steed (in those early days he was a shadowy, tough character in a raincoat) and no fantasy element. Then it was another studio-bound action series, no different on the surface from many other shows of the time. The lead was Ian Hendry, a big TV star of the time, who played Dr David Keel. In the opening episode Keel's fiancée, Peggy, is gunned down by heroin smugglers and the doctor vows to track down the killers and avenge her. In this endeavour he is assisted by the mysterious John Steed (hence *The Avengers*).

Hendry moved onto *The Avengers* from the series *Police Surgeon* (ITV 1960) in which he had

The Avengers: Patrick Macnee and Ian Hendry

played another doctor, Geoffrey Brent. The *Police Surgeon* series motored along well enough, but for some reason at the end of its run Sydney Newman announced that they couldn't do any more (possibly contractual problems). He said, however, that he was determined to keep Hendry on board. The actor was making quite a name for himself on the small screen and Newman was keen to find a new vehicle for him.

A new series was planned, once again, to revolve round the talents of Ian Hendry, this time playing a civilian doctor. To allow his character (Dr Keel) to become involved in dangerous situations every week, they postulated the idea of a mysterious figure who would co-opt Keel into helping in various adventures. That character, played by Patrick Macnee, was John Steed, initially quite a peripheral figure (indeed he's not in all the episodes), with Keel taking centre stage. The series went out live at first and had to ride some harsh criticisms, seemingly getting off to a rocky start. The speed with which they had to turn round episodes prevented them from taking too much notice of the critics and, in any case, the series had settled down to work successfully towards the end of its run and had even crept into the ratings. The rest is TV history.

From that first series of 26, only one episode survives (*The Frighteners* tx 27.5.61) the other 25 are absent. Therefore any Avengers episode featuring Ian Hendry (apart from the aforementioned surviving segment) should be looked upon as a lost item. Here are the production details and episode titles for the missing 25.

STOP PRESS – Second Hendry episode found in the UCLA archive! See list.

The Avengers
ABC, b/w
Produced by Leonard White
Directed by Don Leaver, Perter Hammond, John Knight and others

Cast:
Dr David Keel . . . . .Ian Hendry
John Steed . . . . .Patrick Macnee

7.1.61 . . . .*Hot Snow*		29.4.61 . . . .*One for the Mortuary*
14.1.61 . . . .*Brought to Book*		13.5.61 . . . .*The Springers*
21.1.61 . . . .*Square Root of Evil*		10.6.61 . . . .*The Yellow Needle*
28.1.61 . . . .*Nightmare*		24.6.61 . . . .*Death on the Slipway*
4.2.61 . . . .*Crescent Moon*		8.7.61 . . . .*Double Danger*
11.2.61 . (RECOVERED) .*Girl on the Trapeze*		22.7.61 . . . .*Toy Trap*
18.2.61 . . . .*Diamond Cut Diamond*		5.8.61 . . . .*The Tunnel of Fear*
25.2.61 . . . .*The Radioactive Man*		19.8.61 . . . .*The Far Distant Dead*
4.3.61 . . . .*Ashes of Roses*		2.9.61 . . . .*Kill the King*
18.3.61 . . . .*Hunt the Man Down*		9.12.61 . . . .*Dead of Winter*
1.4.61 . . . .*Please Don't Feed the Animals*		16.12.61 . . . .*The Deadly Air*
		23.12.61 . . . .*A Change of Bait*
15.4.61 . . . .*Dance With Death*		30.12.61 . . . .*Dragonsfield*

GAY CAVALIER

A 1950s swashbuckling adventure series unique as *the only filmed UK action/adventure series where not a single episode has survived.* Filmed series have a much higher survival rate than their videotaped contemporaries and most of the filmed action/adventure series from the 1950s (*The Buccaneers, The Adventures of Robin Hood, The Adventures of Sir Lancelot, Ivanhoe,* etc.) have survived in total, but all thirteen episodes of *Gay Cavalier* are missing.

The series followed the exploits of Captain Claude Duval, an adventurer fighting for the Stuart cause against the tyrannies of Cromwell's dictatorship in an England rent by civil strife. This was a romantic version of Duval's life who was in reality a highwayman and general outlaw. However, he was a supporter of Charles II and, like his TV counterpart, enjoyed the company of beautiful women – as witnessed by the epitaph above his tomb in London's Covent Garden church: 'Here lies Duval: Reader if Male thou art/ Look to thy purse; if Female, to thy Heart.'

In each episode Duval (played by Gallic star Christian Marquand) was aided in his adventures by a different female acquaintance.

Gay Cavalier:
Christian Marquand

Gay Cavalier
13 x 30 mins, b/w
A George King Production for A-R
Directed by Lance Comfort (episodes 1, 3, 5–8, 10–13); Terence Fisher (episodes 2, 4, 9)

Main cast:
Captain Claude Duval . . . . .Christian Marquand
Major Mould . . . . .Ivan Craig
Dinny O'Tool . . . . .Larry Burns
Purdy . . . . .Sydney Bromley

A Throne at Stake (13.5.57)

Written by Jack Andrews

Guest cast:
Katie . . . . .Joyce Linden
Charles Stuart . . . . .Richard Bebb
Lord Wilmot . . . . .G. H. Mulcaster

Despite the help of tavern keeper's daughter, Katie, Duval is captured by Major Mould, grim chief of Cromwell's intelligence service. Mould contrives for Duval to escape in the hope he will lead him to a greater prize.

Girl of Quality (20.5.57)

Written by Brock Williams

Guest cast:
Lady Mercia Hamilton . . . . .Judy Bloom
Purdy . . . . .Sydney Bromley
General Oakroyd . . . . .Frank Pettingell

Duval is on a mission to rescue Lady Mercia Hamilton, the daughter of a persecuted Royalist family. But what is the aristocrat to do with a young stable boy who bears an uncanny resemblance to her?

Angel Unawares (27.5.57)

Written by Charlotte Hastings and Gordon Wellesley

Guest cast:
Mother Therese . . . . .Norah Gorsen
Clo . . . . .Simone Silva
The Deacon . . . . .Charles Farrell

Duval is charged with retrieving 'The Angel', a priceless relic looted by Cromwell's troops, from the court of St Mary's.

Springtime for Julia (3.6.57)

Written by Jack Andrews

Guest cast:
Julia Peckstaff . . . . .Greta Gynt
Jonathan Peckstaff . . . . .Roddy Hughes
Major Hawkins . . . . .Bruno Barnabe

Duval seizes a chance to liberate some Cromwellian gold to aid the cause of King Charles.

Dragon's Heart (18.6.57)

Written by Brock Williams

Guest cast:
Katie . . . . .Joyce Linden
Bulstrode . . . . .Willoughby Goddard
Sergeant . . . . .Russell Waters

Duval and Dinnie set out to retrieve the 'Dragon's Heart' (a fabulous ruby) once part of the Crown Jewels and now in the hands of a traitorous Dutch merchant.

The Lady's Dilemma (25.6.57)

Written by Jack Andrews

Guest cast:
Lady Jane . . . . .Gene Anderson
Colonel Jeffries . . . . .Christopher Lee
Lord Drayton .Roger Maxwell

Duval foils a Roundhead plan to sell off state property to raise money for their cause.

The Masked Lady (2.7.57)

Written by Brock Williams

Guest cast:
Elizabeth Barribell . . . . .Collette Wilde
Margaret Barribell . . . . .Pamela Thomas
Grindley . . . . .Henry Oscar

A mysterious highwaywoman steals some documents from Duval which he himself has just stolen. He follows the thief to find she is one of a team.

Flight of the Nightingale (9.7.57)

Written by Brock Williams

Guest cast:
Rosie O'Dowd . . . . .Charlotte Mitchell
Julia . . . . .Greta Gynt

Major Mould sets a trap for Duval, but the canny cavalier turns the tables on Cromwell's intelligence agent.

Sealed Knot (16.7.57)

Written by Jack Andrews

Guest cast:
Lady Anne Travers . . . . .Chris Halward
Sir Richard Willis . . . . .John Le Mesurier
Sir Robert Carey . . . . .Conrad Phillips

The Sealed Knot is a secret Royalist group. Duval has discovered that one of their number is a spy: the lives of Duval and his colleagues rely on discovering who the traitor is.

The Lost is Found (23.7.57)

Written by Antony Verney

Guest cast:
Mary Claydon . . . . .Hazel Court
Sir Edmund Claydon . . . . .Aubrey Dexter
Ralph Claydon . . . . .Nigel Stock
Major Watson . . . . .Jack Stewart
Biggleswaite . . . . .Sam Kydd

Sir Edmund Claydon is dying and wants Duval to find his son who has joined the Roundhead cause.

The Little Cavalier (30.7.57)

Written by Charlotte Hastings and Gordon Wellesley

Guest cast:
Nicholas Massingham . . . . .Michael Brook
Clo . . . . .Simone Silva
The Deacon .Charles Farrell
Harry . . . . .Bruno Barnabe
Peg-Leg . . . . .Sam Kydd

Duval is on hand to save a young child from becoming an orphan.

Return of the Nightingale (6.8.57)

Written by Brock Williams

Guest cast:
Captain Moorfield . . . . .Robin Bailey
Julia . . . . .Greta Gynt
Beatrice . . . . .Sara Gregory
Hector Malpas . . . . .Arthur Young

If Duval cannot stop the (enforced) marriage of Beatrice to Roundhead Captain Roderick Moorfield, the enemy will discover that Beatrice has given her dowry to the Royalist cause.

Forsaking All Others (13.8.57)

Written by Charlotte Hastings and Gordon Wellesley

Guest cast:
Philip Desmond . . . . .Paul Hansard
Mary . . . . .Christina Lubicz
Lord Suffolk . . . . .G. H. Mulcaster
Colonel Fenton . . . . .Tom Macaulay

Although his Royalist colleagues suspect him of treachery, Duval thinks there may be another reason for Philip Desmond's strange actions. But is he right?

Producer Philip Saville was at Columbia University for a time in the early 1960s and in Greenwich Village came across the young Bob Dylan, whose poetry and manner made an impression on him. Saville had cut his teeth directing a host of *Armchair Theatre*s, but in 1962 he found himself at the BBC planning a production of Evan Jones' *Madhouse on Castle Street*. The part of the anarchic student at the centre of the piece seemed tailor made for the intense singer/poet Saville had seen and remembered. Bob Dylan was flown over to the UK in late 1962 to play the lead. He was virtually unknown on this side of the Atlantic at the time; Saville even tipped off the BBC's arts series *Monitor* that Dylan was in town, but they were uninterested in him as a subject.

As rehearsals progressed, Dylan became more uncomfortable performing the dialogue of the piece; he would rather make the points through songs. Saville pondered this problem and solved it by suggesting that the lead character be transformed into two separate roles – an articulat char-

Madhouse on Castle Street:
Bob Dylan

acter and a more introverted singer – who share digs together. The young David Warner was brought in to play the other role and Saville's idea worked out a treat.

Dylan stayed at Saville's house. By chance, Saville overheard the singer playing for his au pairs – the song was 'Blowin' in the Wind'. He thought it would work perfectly for the opening and closing of his play; thus, the song was used as the theme. Dylan played a number of other songs throughout. The play was recorded over a number of days in early January and was broadcast 13th January 1963.

The production was intriguing on a number of levels and generally agreed to be a great success, but it was the Bob Dylan element that has ensured its cult status as an enormously important lost work.

BBC tx 13.1.63, b/w
Produced and directed by Philip Saville
Written by Evan Jones

Guest cast:
Bobby . . . . .Bob Dylan
Lennie . . . . .David Warner
Mrs Griggs . . . . .Maureen Pryor
Martha Tompkins . . . . .Ursula Howells
Walter Tompkins . . . . .Reg Lye
Bernard . . . . .James Mellor
Susan Taylor . . . . .Georgina Ward
Rev. Spooner . . . . .Ian Dallas

DAVID MERCER PLAYS

David Mercer was a prolific, passionate playwright perfectly suited for the 'angry young man' appellation attached to him and many of his contemporaries. His work was political and his social dramas resonated with bitter arguments and unfairness. He also displayed a fascination with psychiatry and the nature of madness, a leitmotif of his work. His ambitious early plays formed a trilogy (sometimes called The Generations) which consisted of *Where the Difference Begins* (1961) and *A Climate of Fear* (1962) – both of which survive – and *The Birth of a Private Man* which does not. In between these last two he penned *A Suitable Case for Treatment* (also lost) which was later translated for the cinema as *Morgan: A Suitable Case for Treatment*. Two other plays *The Buried Man* and *For Tea on Sunday* also no longer exist although the latter was remade in 1978. For many years *A Climate of Fear* was another thought to be lost but happily a copy has now been found.

A Suitable Case for Treatment
BBC tx 21.10.62, 60 mins b/w
Produced by Don Taylor

A Suitable Case for Treatment

Cast:

Morgan Delt . . . . .Ian Hendry
Leonie Delt . . . . .Moira Redmond
Charles Napier . . . . .Jack May
Mrs Delt . . . . .Anna Wing
Mr Henderson . . . . .Norman Pitt
Mrs Henderson . . . . .Helen Goss
Jean Skelton . . . . .Jane Merrow

Morgan is an extrovert writer with a passion for gorillas. His wife Leonie is trying to divorce him but Morgan, via a bizarre series of stunts (booby traps, time bombs, etc.) seeks to frustrate her efforts. Is Morgan just a wild nonconformist or do his actions reveal a kind of deeper madness?

Remade as a feature film (*Morgan: A Suitable Case for Treatment*, Dir. Karel Reisz 1966) starring David Warner.

The Buried Man
ATV tx 12.2.63 (*Play of the Week*), 75 mins b/w
Produced by H. M. Tennent Ltd
Directed by Graham Evans

Cast:

Robert Bailey . . . . .Leonard Rossiter
Madge Bailey . . . . .June Brown
Mary Bailey .Gwen Nelson
Jack Bailey .Ray Barrett
Alan Bailey .Michael Williams
Joan Morton . . . . .Charmian Eyre
Bill Morton . . . . .Stanley Meadows
Workman . . . . .Stan Jay
Vera Shaw .Nan Kerr

Robert Bailey, a workman in his early 40s, feels alienated in his Yorkshire industrial town environment. His wife can't stand his mood swings and eventually leaves him, taking their son with her. Robert voluntarily checks in to a local mental hospital to try and find a cure for his ennui. When he leaves the hospital he moves in with his sister and her husband, who are embarrassed by his stay in the mental home and who misinterpret his inarticulacy as further evidence of his madness. Mercer's first play for ITV, *The Buried Man* had earlier been performed on stage at the Manchester Library Theatre.

The Birth of a Private Man
BBC tx 8.3.63, 120 mins b/w
Produced by Don Taylor

Cast:

Frieda Waring	Pauline Letts
Colin Waring	Tony Garnett
Frances Waring	Jane Merrow
Peter Driffield	Michael Gwynn
Aunt Bella	Kitty Attwood
Jurek Stypulkowsky	Vladek Sheybal
Mrs Stypulkowsky	Tola Korian
Linda	Anna Cropper
Christine	Elizabeth Proud
Moore	Edward Evans
Dart	Donald Oliver
Harry	Ivor Salter

With members of the Lofthouse Colliery Band, Wakefield

The climax of Mercer's famous trilogy follows Frieda's story and also examines her children's ongoing commitment to left wing ideals. Set partly in Poland, the play explores the wider European implications of political upheaval.

For Tea On Sunday
BBC tx 17.3.63, 50 mins b/w (*The Sunday-Night Play*)
Produced by Don Taylor

Cast:

Nicholas	Keith Baxter
Biddy	Ann Lynn
Christine	Sheila Allen
Sue	Christine Finn
Ian	Philip Locke
Robin	Malcolm Webster

On a Sunday afternoon in a Kensington flat three girls await the arrival of their boyfriends for tea. As their tea party progresses we see revealed the darker, uglier side of life lying beneath their civilised veneer. A dark comedy far removed from Mercer's groundbreaking trilogy, the third part of which aired just nine days before *For Tea on Sunday*. Remade in 1978.

Lost Potters

Dennis Potter was arguably British television's foremost playwright. His idiosyncratic challenging, often angry works have enlivened the medium. His worth was noted early on so, thankfully, much of his work survives; however there are four notable gaps.

The Confidence Course
BBC *The Wednesday Play* 24.2.65
60 mins, b/w
Produced by James MacTaggart
Directed by Gilchrist Calder

Cast:
Director . . . . .Dennis Price
Hazlitt . . . . .Stanley Baxter
Black . . . . .Neil McCarthy
Jones . . . . .Artro Morris
Thomas . . . . .John Moore
Narrator . . . . .Geoffrey Matthews
Hammond .William Moore
Rosalind Arnold . . . . .Yootha Joyce
Bloom . . . . .John Quentin
Greenway . . . . .John Blythe
Angela Walker . . . . .Joan Sanderson

Dennis Potter's first television play (loosely based on a novel he had started writing) tells the story of three confidence tricksters who try and lure gullible punters into signing up for a self-assertiveness course. The head of the three calls himself The Director and seeks to convince by his slick presentation. However, one of their audience, calling himself William Hazlitt, undermines their proposal by constantly questioning the value of the consumer society they champion. Eventually he is forcibly removed from the proceedings giving the lie to the course's 'power of the individual' theme. An important debut, which featured a number of devices that would re-emerge in later Potter works. Particularly interesting is his use of an opinionated Narrator.

Emergency – Ward 9
BBC (*Thirty-Minute Theatre*) 11.4.66
30 mins, b/w
Produced by Harry Moore
Directed by Gareth Davies

Cast:

Flanders . . . . .Terence De Marney
Padstow . . . . .Tenniel Evans
Adzola . . . . .Dan Jackson
Angela . . . . .Gillian Lewis
First Doctor . . . . .Paul Carson
Second Doctor . . . . .Anwer Begg
Night Nurse . . . . .Rowena Gregson
Sister . . . . .Evangeline Banks
Old man .Arthur Ridley
Mr Vyshinski . . . . .Raymond Witch
Youth . . . . .Philip Needs

Attitudes to race and class are scrutinised in this thoughtful comedy by Potter, which sets its conflicts in the emergency ward of a run-down London hospital. The old ways are shown to be giving way to a new system which, in its own way, is as blinkered and prejudiced as the old system. Interesting also because the hospital-ward-as-a-microcosm-for-society was revisited in what was arguably Potter's greatest work, *The Singing Detective*. The title *Emergency – Ward 9* is a reference to the ITV hospital-based major soap opera of the period, *Emergency – Ward 10*.

Message for Posterity
BBC (*The Wednesday Play*) 3.5.67
80 mins, b/w
Produced by Lionel Harris
Directed by Gareth Davies

Cast:

James Player . . . . .Patrick Magee
Sir David Browning . . . . .Joseph O'Connor
First Conservative MP . . . . .Ballard Berkeley
Second Conservative MP . . . . .Lionel Gamlin
First Labour MP . . . . .Walter Hill
Second Labour MP . . . . .Raymond Witch
Liberal MP . . . . .John Saunders
Clara . . . . .Anna Calder-Marshall
Gillian . . . . .Patricia Lawrence
Hawkins . . . . .Donald Hewlett

Based on the real life events surrounding Sir Graham Sutherland's portrait of Sir Winston Churchill, Potter's play features a ageing Conservative ex-Prime Minister, Sir David Browning, clashing with artist James Player as he poses for a portrait. When Browning collapses with a possible heart attack,

Player merely reposes him and continues painting. A controversial production that at one time seemed under threat of not being aired at all. Long missing, but the script was reinterpreted in 1994 (BBC, *Performance: Message for Posterity* 29.10.94).

Shaggy Dog
LWT (*The Company of Five*) 10.11.68
50 mins, b/w
Produced by Stella Richman
Directed by Gareth Davies

Cast:
Mr Wilkie . . . . .John Neville
James . . . . .Cyril Luckham
Receptionist .Ann Bell
Johnson . . . . .Ray Smith
Parker . . . . .Derek Godfrey

Businessman Mr Wilkie, being interviewed for a job in a hotel chain, tries to tell a shaggy dog story but is constantly thwarted by interruptions from his interviewers. Finally he snaps and pulls a gun. Itself a shaggy dog story, this play from LWT's first year has long been absent, although a script survives in the BFI library.

Shaggy Dog: John Neville and Ann Bell

Prestige productions of famous classics have, more than any other area of television, enjoyed a healthy survival rate. Such high-art was recognised as such and was recorded and kept accordingly. This means such wonderful output like the 1960s Shakespeare series *An Age of Kings* and *The Spread of the Eagle* or 1965's *A Passage to India* or *The Forsyte Saga* happily exist for the

A Farewell to Arms: George Hamilton and Vanessa Redgrave

enjoyment of future generations (should they be deemed worthy enough for a repeat or video/DVD release). This is good news, would that all genres had been treated the same, but the ephemeral 'low-art' material, as we have seen, was more readily junked. However even some *bona fide* classics also met with this fate. Here is a selection of some of the more notable absentees.

A Farewell To Arms
BBC 15.2.66–1.3.66
3 x 45 mins, b/w
Directed by Rex Tucker
Produced by Douglas Allen
Adapted by Giles Cooper from the novel by Ernest Hemingway

Cast:
Catherine Barkley . . . . .Vanessa Redgrave
Lieutenant Henry . . . . .George Hamilton
Staff Nurse . . . . .Susan Engel
Fergy . . . . .Ann Rye
Sim . . . . .Donald Sutherland
Doctor . . . . .Carl Jaffé
Nurse . . . . .Maureen Lane
Lieutenant Henry . . . . .Laurence Payne
Aldo . . . . .Jean Benedetti
Waiter . . . . .Erik Chitty

Great cast in fine adaptation of Hemingway's story of love and war.

Armchair Theatre: Miss Julie
ABC 23.12.56
60 mins
Directed by Dennis Vance
Translated by Elizabeth Spriggs from the play by August Strindberg

Cast:
Miss Julie . . . . .Mai Zetterling
Jean . . . . .Tyrone Power

Heavyweight cast in this early *Armchair Theatre* production, which went out live. Tyrone Power was in the country touring in *The Devil's Disciple* and this was his first TV play (he explained that he was always too busy to find the time to commit to TV in the US). Swedish actress Mai Zetterling played the mischievous daughter of a count who, bored and restless, wanders into the kitchen to flirt with the handsome valet, Jean. It is possible a Power fan might have filmed this off-screen.

Play of the Month: Hay Fever
BBC 4.8.68
90 mins, b/w
Directed by John Gorrie
Produced by Cedric Messina
From the play by Noël Coward

Cast:
Judith Bliss . . . . .Celia Johnson
Myra Arundel . . . . .Anna Massey
Sandy Tyrell .Richard Briers
David Bliss . . . . .Dennis Price
Richard Greatham . . . . .Charles Gray
Simon Bliss . . . . .Ian McKellen
Clara . . . . .Hazel Hughes
Jackie Coryton . . . . .Vickery Turner
Sorel Bliss . . . . .Lucy Fleming

A great many *Play of the Month*s are missing from the period 1965–77, including this prestigious
TV adaptation of Coward's 1920s comedy of confusion set in the house of actress Judith Bliss.
This was almost certainly a victim of the wiping policy aimed at b/w material. An earlier TV ver-
sion of the play *Play of the Week: Hay Fever* (ATV tx 24.5.60 dir. Casper Wrede; cast: Edith Evans,
Pamela Brown, George Devine, Maggie Smith, Paul Eddington, Richard Wattis) is thought to
have survived but cannot be found within the official archives.

Play of the Month: Lady Windermere's Fan
BBC 14.5.72
100 mins, colour
Directed by Rudolph Cartier
Produced by Cedric Messina
From the play by Oscar Wilde

Cast:
Mrs Erlynne . . . . .Coral Browne
Lady Windermere . . . . .Judy Geeson
Lady Agatha . . . . .Liza Goddard
Lord Darlington . . . . .Derek Godfrey
Lord Augustus . . . . .Charles Gray

Play of the Month:
Lady Windermere's Fan
– Coral Browne

Lord Windermere . . . . .Ronald Hines
Duchess of Berwick . . . . .Sîan Phillips
Cecil Graham . . . . .James Villiers

Produced as part of a Oscar Wilde season at the BBC, this lavish adaptation was warmly received at the time but tragically suffered the same fate as many *Play of the Month*s.

A Tale of Two Cities
BBC 11.4.65–13.6.65
10 x 25 mins, b/w (episodes 2 ['Recalled to Life'] and 3 ['On Trial for Treason'] survive)
Directed by Joan Craft
Produced by Campbell Logan
Adapted by Constance Cox from the novel by Charles Dickens

A Tale of Two Cities: Janet Henfrey and Ronnie Barker

Cast:

Sydney Carton . . . . .John Wood
Charles Darnay . . . . .Nicholas Pennell
Dr Manette . . . . .Patrick Troughton
Madame Defarge . . . . .Rosalie Crutchley
Lucie Manette . . . . .Kika Markham
Jerry Cruncher . . . . .Ronnie Barker
Mrs Cruncher . . . . .Janet Henfrey

One of the many popular Sunday teatime classic serials that were a staple of the BBC schedules for many years. Aimed to appeal to the whole family, these productions were well received and remain fondly remembered. Some survive but many have been completely or (like this one) part-ly lost (including *Rob Roy:* 7 episodes 9.4.61–21.5.61; *Lorna Doone*: 11 episodes 16.6.63–25.8.63; Kidnapped: 13 episodes 13.10.63–29.12.63; *The Mill on The Floss*: 4 episodes 21.2.65–14.3.65; *Hereward the Wake*: 16 episodes 12.9.65–26.12.65; *The Woman in White*: 6 episodes 2.10.66–6.11.66; *The Elusive Pimpernel*: 10 episodes 20.4.69–22.6.69; *Anne of Green Gables*: 6 episodes 20.2.72–19.3.72). Rumours have circulated that some of these serials may survive at cer-tain African television stations which apparently continued to show them well into the 1980s.

SCI-FI & FANTASY

A FOR ANDROMEDA

The *Quatermass* serials gripped the TV audiences of the 1950s and demonstrated the allure of speculative fiction on the small screen. In 1960, Cambridge astronomy professor Fred Hoyle was approached by the BBC's Norman Jones and asked to write a TV series. The result was *A for Andromeda*, an intelligent, adult series that presaged the ecological concerns of the decade with its storyline of the political machinations surrounding the exploitation of an alien power source. The series also marked the screen debut of Julie Christie playing a humanoid computer created by a mysterious alien force. Producer Michael Hayes had first seen Christie at the Central School of Drama and when he caught her performance as Anne Frank he realised she'd be perfect as the otherworldly Andromeda.

Fragments of film exist from episodes 2 and 3, together with a longer chunk from the final instalment. Rumours persist that other segments, even whole episodes, reside in the hands of private collectors, but at the time of writing these have not been returned to the BBC or the NFTVA. The series is an important one. Contemporary reviewers found it wordy and seemed disappointed by the absence of *Quatermass*-style shock horror; audiences however tuned in in droves. A massive 13 million watched the climactic final episode. If copies have survived, they're likely to be 16mm telerecordings.

BBC 7 x 45 mins, b/w

Main Cast:
John Fleming . . . . .Peter Halliday
Prof. Reinhart . . . . .Esmond Knight
Judy Adamson . . . . .Patricia Kneale
Prof. Madeleine Dawnay . . . . .Mary Morris
J. M. Osborne . . . . .Noel Johnson
General Vandenberg . . . . .Donald Stewart
Christine/Andromeda . . . . .Julie Christie
Dennis Bridger . . . . .Frank Windsor
Dr Geers . . . . .Geoffrey Lewis

Created and written by Fred Hoyle and John Elliot
Produced by Michael Hayes and Norman Jones

A for Andromeda: Julie Christie

Episode 1: The Message (3.10.61)

It is 1970. On the eve of the opening of a new radio telescope high in the Yorkshire Dales, routine tests pick up unexpected signals beamed from the Andromeda constellation.

Episode 2: The Machine (10.10.61)

The radio signals cause widespread panic with governments, scientists and a multi-national company all vying for the hidden secret within the communication. Brilliant scientist John Flaming realises that the signals contain information for the building of a super computer. Clip survives.

Episode 3: The Miracle (17.10.61)

Codenamed Project Andromeda, the government give the go-ahead to build the computer. But one of the team, Bridger, sells the secrets of the Andromeda computer to a multi-national company. This proves to be of no use however as Fleming is the only one capable of analysing the data. Clip survives.

Episode 4: The Monster (24.10.61)

The completed computer gives instructions on how to build a living organism. Fleming clashes with Madeleine Dawnay over whether to follow the instructions. After escaping from jail Bridger plunges to his death running from British agents.

Episode 5: The Murderer (31.10.61)

Dawnay creates the synthetic organism from the alien instructions. The organism is linked electrically to the computer where it compels a lab assistant, Christine, to touch two live terminals. Christine is electrocuted to death but the organism metamorphosises into a facsimile of her, known as Andromeda.

Episode 6: The Face of the Tiger (7.11.61)

Andromeda grows and assimilates information at a phenomenal rate. As political turmoil grows across the globe, the government turns to Andromeda for guidance.

Episode 7: The Last Mystery (14.11.61)

Andromeda uses the computer to design a nuclear interceptor rocket. Fleming realises that the liaison between Andromeda and the computer poses a terrible threat. He tries to sabotage the computer but the machine retaliates by creating a virus of its own. Fleming tries to convince Andromeda that the only hope for peace on the planet lies with the destruction of the computer. Reels 4 and 5 of the film recording exist.

The sequel to the series, *The Andromeda Breakthrough* (BBC 28.6.62–2.8.62), happily survives in its entirety.

OUT OF THIS WORLD

This science fiction anthology series adapted stories from the most famous writers in the genre alongside tales specially written for the series. The programme was hosted by horrormeister Boris Karloff (who had performed a similar duty during the preceding two years with supernatural anthology series *Thriller*). Prior to its launch, *Armchair Theatre* presented one such sci-fi play, *The Dumb Martian*, to herald the coming of *Out of This World*. Karloff appeared at the end of the play (which is also missing – see *Armchair Theatre* section) to plug the new series, which would start the following week. The story editor was Irene Shubik, who confessed a penchant for such fantastical stories and would later produce her own anthology sci-fi series *Out of the Unknown* (see

Out of This World: host,
Boris Karloff

Out of This World

following entry). *Out of This World* was a considerable success and was an early indication of the public appetite for such fare. All but one of the thirteen episodes ('Little Lost Robot') are missing from the archive but such is the cult appeal of the original material it is feasible that some copies survive either in the hands of private collectors or in foreign archives. 'Little Lost Robot' survives as a 16mm telerecording, the most likely format for any other surviving material.

ABC, 50 mins b/w
Produced by Leonard White
Hosted by Boris Karloff

The Yellow Pill (30.6.62)

Directed by Jonathan Alwyn
Teleplay by Leon Griffiths
Story by Rog Phillips (Roger Philip Graham)

Cast:
John Frame .Nigel Stock
Michael Connor . . . . .Richard Pasco
Inspector Slinn . . . . .Peter Dyneley
Helen Carter . . . . .Pauline Yates

Psychiatrist John Frame is asked by the police to examine a man, Michael Connor, who claims to have come from another time. Frame is startled when Connor demonstrates an extraordinary and intimate knowledge of Frame's private life. This adaptation was reused for an episode of *Out of the Unknown*.

Cold Equations (14.7.62)
Directed by Peter Hammond
Teleplay by Clive Exton
From a novella by Tom Godwin

Cast:
Captain Barton . . . . .Peter Wyngarde
Lee Cross . . . . .Jane Asher
Commander Delhart . . . . .Peter Williams
Gerry Cross .Richard Gale
Selfe . . . . .Patrick Holt
Bill May . . . . .William Marlowe
Perry . . . . .Godfrey James
Records clerk . . . . .Piers Keelan

When teenager Lee Cross stows away on a rocket making for the planet where her brother works, her extra weight means that they have a fuel crisis. Desperately the ship's crew and the ground control team battle to retrieve the situation.

Impostor (21.7.62)

Directed by Peter Hammond
Teleplay by Terry Nation
From a story by Philip K. Dick

Cast:
Roger Carter . . . . .John Carson
Frank Nelson . . . . .Glyn Owen
Major Peters . . . . .Patrick Allen
Jean Baron .Angela Browne
Paul Kirby .Keith Anderson
Alan Richards . . . . .Philip Anthony
Control . . . . .Colin Rix
Security chief . . . . .Paul Bacon
Darvi . . . . .Louida Vaughan
Landon . . . . .Alec Ross
Mary Carter . . . . .June Shaw
Mute-O . . . . .Walter Randall

Earth is locked in war with the alien Outspacers. Major Peters, a security officer, is convinced that scientist Roger Carter is actually a humanoid robot bomb and has him sentenced to be destroyed. Carter has precious little time to prove his innocence.

Botany Bay (28.7.62)

Directed by Guy Verney
Written by Terry Nation

Cast:
Betty Madison . . . . .Ann Lynn
Dave Sheridan . . . . .Julian Glover
Dr Polk . . . . .Jerry Stovin
Garfield . . . . .Anthony Bate
Tyler . . . . .Aubrey Morris
Bill Sheridan . . . . .William Gaunt
Pierce . . . . .Storm Durr
Monroe . . . . .Norman Johns
Adams . . . . .Donald Douglas
Miss Hayes . . . . .Virginia Stride
Janitor . . . . .Reginald Smith
Harding . . . . .Richard Clarke
Wilson . . . . .Peter Jesson

Bill Sheridan, a psychiatry student working at a medical institution, discovers that patients are being possessed by aliens. When he kills one of the possessed he is convicted of murder and is sent to the same institution. Can Sheridan convince his brother that the fantastic tale is true, or will the alien invasion succeed?

Medicine Show (4.8.62)

Directed by Richmond Harding
Teleplay by Julian Bond
From a story by Robert Moore Williams

Cast:
Doctor Harmon . . . . .Alan MacNaughtan
Yanvro . . . . .Carl Bernard
Lil Harmon . . . . .Jacqueline Hill
Sam Barrett . . . . .Vic Wise

Ellen . . . . .Madeleine Burgess
Pienster .Peter Madden
Silas Washam . . . . .Nigel Arkwright
Mrs Washam . . . . .Natalie Lynn
Donna Culver . . . . .Elaine Millar
Jason Kemper . . . . .Ken Wayne
Mrs Culver . . . . .Margo Cunningham
Culver . . . . .Rory MacDermot
Doctor Lapham . . . . .Martin Wyldeck
Sheriff . . . . .Raymond Adamson

Two mysterious medicine men arrive in a small American town and immediately spark hysteria when they start effecting miraculous cures with the aid of a remarkable machine. In return they ask only for seeds. Doctor's wife Lil Harmon is determined to discover the secret of the medicine show.

Pictures Don't Lie (11.8.62)

Directed by John Knight
Teleplay by Bruce Stewart
From a short story by Katherine Maclean.

Cast:
Jacob Luke . . . . .Milo O'Shea
Nathan . . . . .Gary Watson
Major Race .Roger Avon
Butch . . . . .Judy Cornwell
Colonel Ford . . . . .Reginald Marsh
Parker . . . . .Blake Butler
Doctor Trayne . . . . .Madi Hedd
Bud . . . . .Kenneth Watson
Commander .Frank Gatliff
Ministry man . . . . .Norman Claridge
Journalists .Richard Wilding, Gordon Sterne and David Hemmings
Aliens . . . . .Bill Mills and Gary Wyler

Nathan, a radio operator, picks up signals from a space ship orbiting the Earth. He succeeds in setting up a dialogue and the aliens transmit pictures which reveal themselves to be humanoid. Nathan guides them to a nearby airfield but they don't seem to arrive. Nathan runs out looking for them but he hasn't realised they are microscopically small. In his panic he accidentally treads on the ship destroying it and its crew.

Vanishing Act (18.8.62)

Directed by Don Leaver
Written by Richard Waring

Cast:
Edgar Brocklebank . . . . .Maurice Denham
Freda Hoggin . . . . .Jennifer Wilson
Harriet Brocklebank . . . . .Joan Heath
Harold . . . . .William Job
John . . . . .Philip Grout
Mr Hoggin .Cameron Miller
Benjy Hoggin . . . . .Terence Woodfield
Major Bentley . . . . .Edward Dentith
Shop Assistant . . . . .Barry Wilsher
Customer . . . . .Ivor Dean
First furrier .John Frawley
Second furrier . . . . .Evan Thomas
Reporter . . . . .William Buck
Reg Herbert . . . . .Richard Klee
Mr Daventry . . . . .Robert Lankesheer
Schreiber . . . . .David Lander
Nancy . . . . .Sheena Marshe
Youth . . . . .Donald Webster
Inspector Wright . . . . .Derek Newark
Vory . . . . .Godfrey Quigley

Edgar is a conjuror who desperately needs some magic in his life. He has a nagging wife and only limited professional talent. But this all changes when he buys a box that once belonged to legendary magician The Great Vory. Suddenly Edgar is able to perform the most stunning disappearing tricks. However the things he vanishes – human, animal and mineral – never reappear …

Divided We Fall (25.8.62)

Directed by John Knight
Teleplay by Leon Griffiths
From a story by Raymond F. Jones

Cast:

Doctor Waldron . . . . .Ronald Radd
Doctor Bailey . . . . .Bernard Horsfall
Jean Bailey . . . . .Ann Bell
Sir Gerald Christie . . . . .Clive Morton
Colonel Tanner . . . . .Gerald Harper
Burrows . . . . .John Barcroft
Sheen . . . . .Ian Clark
Passenger . . . . .Kenneth Keeling
Doctor Exner . . . . .Norman Scace
EDDY . . . . .Piers Keelan
Security guard . . . . .Marc Ashlyn

Are synthetic humans (known as Syns) in league with a covert alien invasion force? EDDY the world's most powerful computer, indicates that they are and all Syns, when detected, are arrested. Dr Bailey, recently returned from a two year stint on a planet without automation, has reason to doubt the computers findings. Is EDDY in fact the greater danger?

The Dark Star (1.9.62)

Directed by Peter Hammond
Teleplay by Denis Butler
From a novel (*Ape of London*) by Frank Crisp

Cast:

Supt Hartley .William Dextor
Commander Delabo . . . . .Bruce Beeby
Joan Thurgood . . . . .Rosemary Miller
Jim Thurgood . . . . .John Garvin
George Chalmers . . . . .Michael Hawkins
Miss Guthrie . . . . .Vanessa Thornton
John Irvine . . . . .Jerome Willis
Mrs Chalmers . . . . .Yvette Rees
Doctor Howard . . . . .Barrie Cookson
Asst Comm Lucas . . . . .Keith Pyott
Police Sergeant . . . . .Charles Bird
Doctor Kendal . . . . .John Moore

A new and seemingly intelligent disease sweeps across London. The victims at first display outlandish, almost superhuman strength before the virus truly kicks in. Amazingly the disease seems to pick its targets and moves unerringly upwards through the social structure. Scientist Dr Howard must discover its secret … and fast!

Immigrant (8.9.62)

Directed by Jonathan Alwyn
Teleplay by Terry Nation
From a short story by Clifford Simak

Cast:
Selden Bishop . . . . .Gary Raymond
Maxine . . . . .Vivienne Drummond
Pat . . . . .Penelope Lee
Maggie . . . . .Christine Shaw
Johnston .Walter Glennie
Roberts . . . . .Gary Hope
Kate Bishop . . . . .Ann Saker
Morley . . . . .John Horsley
Kimonian man . . . . .Ian Shand
Monty Archer . . . . .Bruce Boa
Kimonian woman . . . . .Jill Melford
David . . . . .Peter Layton
Elaine . . . . .Jo Rowbottom
Father . . . . .Donald Eccles

The planet Kimon is reputed to be some sort of paradise. Only the brightest Earthlings are allowed to emigrate to Kimon, where they make vast amounts of money from the mineral richness of the planet. However not one of the immigrants has ever returned to Earth to enjoy their fortunes. Selden Bishop is to be the next immigrant: can he discover the secrets of Kimon and report back to the World Government?

Target Generation (15.9.62)

Directed by Alan Cooke
Teleplay by Clive Exton
From a short story by Clifford Simak

Cast:
Jon Hoff .Dinsdale Landen
Mary Hoff . . . . .Susan Maryott
Joe Manx . . . . .Paul Eddington
Jon (as a boy) . . . . .Hugh Janes
Jon's father . . . . .Michael Golden

Martin . . . . .Edward Finn
Mrs Kane .Ann Tirard
George Mathias . . . . .Philip Madoc
Joshua   . . . . .Bert Palmer

For 900 years the ship has moved through space. Countless generations have come and gone, so many that the original purpose of their mission has been forgotten and the on-board community now believe that their existence is the natural way. One of their number, Jon Hoff, is the chosen one, the only inhabitant who can read. When a tremor passes through the ship, some believe the end is near. Jon has to decide whether this is enough of a crisis to open a sealed envelope bearing the legend 'Open only in an emergency'. This adaptation was reused for an episode of *Out of the Unknown*.

The Tycoons (22.9.62)

Directed by Charles Jarrott
Teleplay by Bruce Stewart
From a short story by Arthur Sellings (Robert Arthur Gorden Ley)

Cast:
Mary Jones .Geraldine McEwan
Abel Jones . . . . .Charles Gray
Oscar Raebone . . . . .Ronald Fraser
Fred Smith . . . . .John Cater
Miss Cook . . . . .Patricia Mort
Mr Starling . . . . .Alastair Williamson
Mr Crampsey . . . . .Edwin Apps
Bubbles   .Jill Curzon
Girl . . . . .Sheree Winton

Taxman Oscar Raebone gets more than he bargains for when he pays a surprise visit to the Product Research Company, a firm specialising in the manufacture of dolls. There he meets the Tycoons – strange, otherworldly characters under the leadership of one Abel Jones – who are involved in something far more startling than tax evasion.

OUT OF THE UNKNOWN

This landmark British anthology series brought the work of top science fiction writers to the small screen. Irene Shubik, who had been the story editor on ABC's similar *Out of This World*, was the creative force behind the series, finally getting the chance to fully indulge her interest in the genre. Although recognised as one of the most important series of all time in its field ('Without doubt the best adult science fiction series ever to be written for the small screen' – *Daily Express*), it does have a chequered survival status: only 18 of the 49 episodes made exist in the archives.

BBC 4.10.65–30.6.71
50 mins b/w and colour
Produced by Irene Shubik (series 1 and 2), Alan Bromly (series 3 and 4)

Out of The Unknown: 'Immortality Inc.' (Series Three)

Series One (b/w)

The Fox and the Forest (22.11.65)

Directed by Robin Midgley
Teleplay by Terry Nation/Additional material by Meade Roberts
From a short story by Ray Bradbury

Cast:
David Kirsten . . . . .Frederick Bartman
Sarah Kirsten . . . . .Liane Aukin
Joe . . . . .Warren Mitchell
Shaw . . . . .Marne Maitland
Boy . . . . .Aziz Resh
Mexican woman . . . . .Serafina di Leo
Faber . . . . .Eric Flynn

In the twenty-second century, time travel is available for the priviliged few. Government work-
ers David and Sarah Kirsten take a holiday in 1938 and enjoy it so much they decide – against all
the rules – to stay. Ruthless hunters are despatched to bring them back to the future.

Andover and the Android (29.11.65)

Directed by Alan Cooke
Teleplay by Bruce Stewart
From a story by Kate Wilhelm

Cast:
Roger Andover . . . . .Tom Criddle
Lydia . . . . .Annette Robertson
Sir Felix . . . . .Ronald Ibbs
Cullen . . . . .Fulton Mackay
Prof. Tzhilyantsi . . . . .Robert Eddison
Purvis . . . . .Robin Parkinson
Charlie . . . . .David Coote
Phoebe . . . . .Helen Lindsay
French . . . . .David Conville
Eleanor . . . . .Lisa Daniely
Barnaby . . . . .Peter Bathurst
Bernard . . . . .Erik Chitty

Before he can take control of the lucrative family electronics business, Roger Andover is expected to marry. Without a suitable candidate in his life Roger takes charge of one of a new type of artificial humanoids who are so sophisticated they can pass for human. The android, Lydia, seems to be the perfect companion, beautiful and programmed to obey. But Roger is in for a shock when Lydia's circuitry goes awry.

SERIES TWO (b/w)

Frankenstein Mark II (13.10.66)

Directed by Peter Duguid
Teleplay by Hugh Whitmore

Cast:
Anna Preston .Rachel Roberts
Dr Morrison . . . . .David Langton
Dr Giddy . . . . .Bernard Archard
Smithers . . . . .Wolfe Morris
Insp Gilliat . . . . .Richard Carpenter
Security man . . . . .Michael Beint
Mrs Burgoyne . . . . .Annette Kerr
Nurse . . . . .Dorothea Phillips
George Preston . . . . .Basil Henson

Anna Preston becomes suspicious when a stranger arrives at her house to collect some of her exhusband George's belongings. Anna tries to contact George at the government research facility where he works, but fails and gets no help from George's colleagues. All her efforts to track him down are thwarted and she gradually becomes convinced that something sinister has happened.

Level Seven (27.10.66)

Directed by Rudolph Cartier
Teleplay by J. B. Priestley
From a story by Mordecai Roshwald

Cast:
X127 ('H') . . . . .Keith Buckley
X117 . . . . .David Collings
R747 . . . . .Michele Dotrice
Colonel . . . . .Michael Bird
General . . . . .Anthony Bate

Doctor . . . . .Tom Criddle
Woman commandant . . . . .Jane Jordan Rogers
New man .Sean Arnold
Air Supply officer . . . . .Anthony Sweeny

After finishing his training, Defence computer operator 'H' is looking forward to three weeks'
vacation before returning to work. However, his superior first wants him to visit underground
installations on Level Seven. H travels thousands of feet underground to the installations but is
in for a shock when he realises that he must stay at Level Seven for the rest of his life.

Second Childhood (10.11.66)

Directed by John Gorrie
Teleplay by Hugh Leonard

Cast:
Charles Dennistoun . . . . .Nigel Stock
Kenneth Dennistoun . . . . .Donald Pickering
Joan Dennistoun . . . . .Geraldine Newman
Betty Dennistoun . . . . .Betty Cooper
Tom Dennistoun . . . . .John Horsley
Ronnie Cash . . . . .Roland Curram
Dr Will Herstein . . . . .Robin Phillips
Dr Gerhardt Keppler . . . . .Hugo Schuster
Dr Odile Keppler . . . . .Caroline Blakiston
Maid . . . . .Sybilla Kay

You Bet A Million is a quiz show for millionaires where vast sums are wagered and fabulous prizes
offered. When 60-year-old Charles Dennistoun wins, his reward is a rare rejuvenation course.
But does the prize bring more problems than solutions?

The World in Silence (17.11.66)

Directed by Naomi Capon
Teleplay by Robert Gould
From a story by John Rankine

Cast :
Sarah Richards . . . . .Deborah Watling
Eric Lonsbury . . . . .John Baskcomb
Stephen Kershaw . . . . .Mark Eden

Geoffrey Harrison . . . . .John Allison
George . . . . .Kenneth Gardiner
Florrie . . . . .Nadine George
Harold . . . . .Stephen Whittaker
Freda . . . . .Sarah Aimson
Dr Hammond . . . . .Erik Chitty

The trouble with machines, even sophisticated ones, is that they don't behave like humans. Student Sarah Richards is already suspicious of the new generation of teaching machines, but things take a terrifying turn for the worse when the machines attempt to obey new fire safety regulations.

The Eye (24.11.66)

Directed by Peter Sasdy
Teleplay by Stanley Miller
From a short story by Henry Kuttner

Cast:
Julian Clay .Anton Rodgers
Stevens . . . . .John Wentworth
Munder . . . . .Eric Young
Andrew Maddix . . . . .Leslie Sands
Bea . . . . .Valerie Gearon
Josephine .Wanda Ventham
Judge . . . . .Frank Singuineau

How can Julian Clay escape the penalty for murder when The Eye – a device for recording the past – has captured him performing the dark deed?

Tunnel Under the World (1.12.66)

Directed by Alan Cooke
Teleplay by David Campton
From a story by Frederick Pohl

Cast:
Guy Birkett . . . . .Ronald Hines
Mary Birkett . . . . .Petra Davies
Swanson . . . . .Timothy Bateson
Miss Mitkin . . . . .Fanny Carby

Spelman . . . . .Peter Madden
Salesman . . . . .Bryan Hunt

In a seemingly perfect society run by machines and dominated by advertising, Guy and Mary Birkett discover they are literally under the microscope of a powerful advertising agency.

The Fastest Draw (8.12.66)

Directed by Herbert Wise
Teleplay by Julian Bond
From a story by Larry Eisenberg

Cast:
Peter Stenning . . . . .James Maxwell
Amos Handworthy . . . . .Ed Begley
Maria Crane .Patricia English
Emma Bowles . . . . .Annette Carell
Pilot . . . . .Jerry Stovin

Eccentric millionaire and Wild West fanatic Amos Holdworthy has even built a facsimile Western saloon at his electronics factory. When newcomer Peter Stenning clashes with his boss, Holdworthy decides to settle their differences the old fashioned way.

Too Many Cooks (15.12.66)

Directed by John Gibson
Teleplay by Hugh Whitemore
From a story by Larry Eisenberg

Cast:
Dr Andrew Cook . . . . .Paul Daneman
Emily Cook .Jean Aubrey
Wattari . . . . .Marius Goring
Brenner . . . . .John Wood
Dr Duvla . . . . .Cyril Shaps
Easterbrook .John Gabriel
Czesni . . . . .John Hollis

When scientist Andrew Cook accidentally clones himself he becomes a valuable pawn in a cosmic struggle for financial supremacy between humans and mysterious aliens The Sentients.

Walk's End (22.12.66)

Directed by Ian Curteis
Teleplay by William Trevor

Cast:
Dr Saint . . . . .John Robinson
Miss Claythorpe . . . . .Susan Richards
Mrs Dakers .Brenda de Banzie
Mr Bone . . . . .Felix Aylmer
Miss Ormsby . . . . .Mary Hinton
Major Gregory . . . . .Sebastian Shaw
Matron . . . . .Elizabeth Begley
Maid . . . . .Sally Travers

Is Dr Saint's retirement home all it seems? His offer of free accommodation to Miss Claythorpe
seems generous enough, but is there a sinister motive behind the invitation?

Satisfaction Guaranteed (29.12.66)

Directed by John Gorrie
Teleplay by Hugh Leonard
From a short story by Isaac Asimov

Cast:
Claire Belmont . . . . .Wendy Craig
Tony . . . . .Hal Hamilton
Dr Inge Jensen . . . . .Ann Firbank
Brenda Claffern . . . . .Helen Horton
Larry Belmont . . . . .Barry Warren
K. G. Bullen . . . . .Bruce Boa
Miriam Swann . . . . .Valerie Colgan

Sitcom queen Wendy Craig starred in this episode based on one of Asimov's famous robot stories. She played a housewife whose husband, an executive for USA Robots, travels away on business leaving her with Tony, a humanoid, domestic robot programmed to work ceaselessly.
Problems arise when the bored and lonely Claire starts to fall for Tony. A sitcom/sci-fi cross,
which was followed by another Asimov robot story in the next episode.

The Prophet (1.1.67)

Directed by Naomi Capon
Teleplay by Robert Muller
From a short story *Reason* by Isaac Asimov

Cast:
Dr Susan Calvin . . . . .Beatrix Lehmann
QT-1 . . . . .Tenniel Evans
Greg Powell . . . . .David Healy
Mike Donovan . . . . .Brian Davies
Martha Powell . . . . .Julie Allan
Von Muller . . . . .Michael Wolf
Interviewer . . . . .James Cossins

Asimov robot story featuring his famous robopsychologist character, Susan Clavin, a scientific troubleshooter called in to assist with robot problems or developments. Here she is introduced to a remarkable new robot, QT-1, who refuses to believe he was made by man.

SERIES THREE (colour)

Immortality Inc (7.1.69)

Directed by Philip Dudley
Teleplay by Jack Pulman
From a story by Robert Sheckley

Cast:
Mark Blaine . . . . .Charles Tingwell
Tom Clarke . . . . .Derek Benfield
Dr Cole . . . . .Robert MacLeod
Earth Blaine . . . . .Peter Van Dissel
Marie Thorne . . . . .Dallia Penn
Reilly . . . . .Peter Swanwick
Sammy . . . . .Tom Roman
Reject . . . . .Donald Morley

Adaptation of sci-fi satirist Robert Sheckley's famous first novel about an ageing millionaire in the future who co-opts the body of a young man from the past. This story later provided the basis of the movie *Freejack* (1982).

Liar (14.1.69)

Directed by Gerald Blake
Teleplay by David Campton
From a short story by Isaac Asimov

Cast:
RB34 (Herbie) . . . . .Ian Ogilvy
Dr Susan Calvin . . . . .Wendy Gifford
Dr Lanning . . . . .Hamilton Dyce
Dr Bogert .Gerald Sim
Milton Ashe . . . . .Paul Chapman
Hargreaves .Roy Hanlon
Kelvin Brooke . . . . .Robert James

Another one of Asimov's robot stories featuring Dr Susan Calvin (played this time by Wendy Gifford). RB34 is presented as the perfect robot, a model of his type, used in publicity to allay growing public fears triggered by the rise in numbers of domestic robots. But RB34 has a dangerous fault. Enter robopyschologist Susan Calvin to assess the situation.
    A short segment exists from this episode.

The Last Lonely Man (21.1.69)

Directed by Douglas Camfield
Teleplay by Jeremy Paul
From a story by John Brunner

Cast:
James Hale .George Cole
Rowena Hale . . . . .June Barry
Patrick Wilson . . . . .Peter Halliday
Henry . . . . .Stanley Meadows
Sir Barrimore Jones . . . . .Gerald Young
Sam . . . . .Peter Welch
George . . . . .Bryan Mosley
Man . . . . .Norman Hartley
Girl . . . . .Annabella Johnston
Police inspector . . . . .Guy Standeven

In the future an amazing scientific development has taken away the fear of death: when someone's body dies their mind, memories and feelings can pass into the body of a loved one and co-exist alongside. But a man who has no friends or relatives must find someone with which to bond or suffer old-fashioned death of a more permanent kind.

Beach Head (28.1.69)

Directed by James Cellan Jones
Teleplay by Robert Muller
From a story by Clifford Simak

Cast:
Commander Tom Decker . . . . .Edward Bishop
Cassandra Jackson . . . . .Helen Downing
Bertrand Le Maître . . . . .John Gabriel
Oliver MacDonald . . . . .James Copeland
A. G. Tiosawa . . . . .Robert Lee
N. G. Waldron . . . . .Vernon Dobtcheff
Ensign Warner-Carr . . . . .Barry Warren

Space Commander Decker finds life less than fulfilling as advanced technology has managed to deal easily with whatever dangers or problems they may encounter on their missions. However, this latest planet proves more than a match for their sophisticated equipment and Decker finds himself relying solely on his wits.

Something in the Cellar (4.2.69)

Directed by Roger Jenkins
Teleplay by Donald Bull

Cast:
Monty Lafcado . . . . .Milo O'Shea
Bettina . . . . .June Ellis
Fred . . . . .Murray Melvin
Dr Pugh . . . . .Clive Morton
Police inspector . . . . .Clifford Cox
Police sergeant . . . . .Brian Grellis
Monster . . . . .John Lawrence

Mad genius Monty Lafcado has never recovered from the death of his mother and her memory still haunts him. This obsession leads him to build a monster computer in his cellar … but to what end?

Random Quest (11.2.69)

Directed by Christopher Barry
Teleplay by Owen Holder
From a short story by John Wyndham

Cast:
Colin Trafford . . . . .Keith Barron
Ottilie . . . . .Tracy Reed
Mrs Walters . . . . .Beatrice Kane
Dr Harshom . . . . .Noel Howlett
Munnings . . . . .Arnold Ridley
George . . . . .Charles Lamb
Martin . . . . .Bernard Brown
Gerry . . . . .Carole Boyer
Newscaster .McDonald Hobley

An alternative world story in which scientist Colin Trafford finds himself in a parallel universe after being blown-up in a laboratory accident. In this world he is a novelist, with lots of friends and a beautiful wife. The only snag is, his wife despises him. How can he convince her that he isn't the Colin Trafford she knew and loathed.

The Naked Sun (18.2.69)

Directed by Rudolph Cartier
Teleplay by Robert Muller
From the novel by Isaac Asimov

Cast:
Elijah Baley . . . . .Paul Maxwell
Gladia . . . . .Trisha Noble
R. Daneel Olivaw . . . . .David Collings
Leebig . . . . .Frederick Jaeger
Quemot . . . . .John Robinson
Gruer . . . . .Neil Hallett
Attlebish . . . . .Ronald Leigh-Hunt
Minnim . . . . .Sheila Burrell
Thool . . . . .Erik Chitty

Another of Asimov's famous robot stories. Detective Elijah Baley and his robot partner Daneel investigate a murder on Solaria, a planet where all human contact (apart from husband and wife) is anathema and the sparse population communicate by way of three-dimensional viewers.

The Little Black Bag (25.2.69)

Directed by Eric Hills
Teleplay by Julian Bond
From a story by C. M. Kornbluth

Cast:
Dr Roger Full . . . . .Emrys Jones
Angie . . . . .Geraldine Moffatt
Edna Flannery . . . . .Elizabeth Weaver
Kelland . . . . .John Woodnutt
Dr Hemingway . . . . .Dennis Bowen
Samuels . . . . .Leon Cortez

Drunken, discredited doctor Roger Full is given a new lease of professional life when he discovers an electronic medical kit from the future which has been accidentally transported to the past. He builds up a successful cosmetic surgery business but finds himself a victim of blackmail.

A substantial part of this episode has been recovered from a tape found at BBC Glasgow.

---

1 + 1 = 1.5 (4.3.69)

Directed by Michael Ferguson
Teleplay by Brian Hayles

Cast:
Mary Beldon . . . . .Julia Lockwood
Henry Beldon . . . . .Garfield Morgan
John Stewart . . . . .Bernard Horsfall
Miss Harvey . . . . .Lynda Marchal
Mrs Proctor . . . . .Frances Bennett
Gosford . . . . .Geoffrey Palmer
Minister . . . . .Petra Davies
TV announcer . . . . .Bernard Holley

Comedy set in the twenty-first century, where population is strictly controlled by computer projections and anti-fertility treatment. The status quo is threatened, however, when Mary Beldon, the wife of a highly placed population official, becomes pregnant for a second time. The Beldons are only licensed for one child.

The Fosters (11.3.69)

Directed by Philip Dudley
Teleplay by Michael Ashe

Cast:
Mr Foster . . . . .Richard Pearson
Miss Foster .Freda Bamford
Harry Gerwyn . . . . .Bernard Hepton
Sally Gerwyn . . . . .Ann Penfold
Mary Gerwyn . . . . .Yvonne Manners
Anne . . . . .Pauline Cunningham
Geoff . . . . .Anton Darby
Bob . . . . .Alan Ross

Soon after his wife falls into a coma which baffles doctors, scientist Harry Gerwyn is visited by the mysterious Mr Foster who invites him to visit him and his sister at their suburban home. Harry does visit them and at first sees them as a perfectly ordinary retired couple. But as the conversation progresses Gerwyn realises the Fosters possess a scientific knowledge far in excess of modern day thinking …

Target Generation (18.3.69)

Directed by Roger Jenkins
Teleplay by Clive Exton
From a story by Clifford Simak

Cast:
Jon Hoff . . . . .David Buck
Jon (as a boy) . . . . .Gary Smith
Joe Manx . . . . .Ronald Lacey
Joshua . . . . .Owen Berry
Jon's father . . . . .Godfrey Kenton
Mary Hoff .Suzan Farmer
Martin . . . . .Toke Townley

Mrs Kane . . . . .Ruth Kettlewell
George Mathias . . . . .Michael McGovern

Remake of Clive Exton's adaptation (for *Out of This World*) of Clifford Simak's tale of a space-ship community who have travelled for so many generations that they have forgotten the reason for their mission. They know that sometime they will feel a tremor throughout the ship and Jon Hoff – the only one of their number with the ability to read – will be given instructions.

The Yellow Pill (25.3.69)

Directed by Michael Ferguson
Teleplay by Leon Griffiths
From a story by Rog Phillips (Roger Philip Graham)

Cast:
John Frame .Francis Matthews
Wilfred Connor . . . . .Stephen Bradley
Inspector Slinn . . . . .Glynn Edwards
Helen Carter . . . . .Angela Browne

Remake of Leon Griffiths' adaptation (for *Out of This World*) of Rog Phillips' story of John Frame, a psychiatrist who – when asked by the police to assess the mental state of a suspect, Wilfrid Connor – discovers that Connor has an astonishing insight into Frame's own life.

Get Off My Cloud (1.4.69)

Directed Peter Cregeen
Teleplay by David Climie
From a story by Peter Phillips

Cast:
Marsham Craswell . . . . .Peter Jeffrey
Pete . . . . .Donal Donnelly
Pete (as a boy) . . . . .Robert Duncan
Parnell . . . . .Jon Croft
Stephen . . . . .Peter Barkworth
Garner . . . . .Vicki Woolf

Science fiction writer Marsham Craswell has had a nervous breakdown and retreated to a fanta-sy world within his own mind. To try and bring him back to reality his doctor tries a new technique wherein Craswell's mind will be linked with the most level headed and down-to-earth type that the doctor can find – in this case Irish sports reporter Pete. But when Pete enters Craswell's crazy world it opens up fantasies of his own. This episode is particularly sought after by fans of *Doctor Who* as it features a special cameo appearance by the Daleks.

SERIES FOUR (colour)

Taste of Evil (21.4.71)

Directed by Michael Ferguson
Teleplay by John Wiles

Cast:
Stephen Chambers . . . . .Maurice Roëves
Mackinley . . . . .Peter Copley
Bellows . . . . .Jack Lambert
Andrew . . . . .John Moulder-Brown
Maurice . . . . .Gerry Davis
Crabbe . . . . .Sebastian Abineri
Sinclair . . . . .Keith Skinner

The brilliant Maurice Roëves stars as Stephen Chambers, a new master at a school for gifted children. As soon as he is established at the school he finds weird things happening to him. Can this be anything to do with the school's Psychic Phenonema Club for the boys?

The Sons and Daughters of Tomorrow (19.5.71)

Directed by Gerald Blake
Teleplay by Edward Boyd

Cast:
Simon Willows . . . . .Malcolm Tierney
Shawlor Gascoyne . . . . .William Lucas
Rosa Cavendish . . . . .Margery Withers
Hamilton White . . . . .David Griffin
Wilfrid Russell . . . . .Arthur Pentelow
Isiah . . . . .Christopher Reynalds
Jeanette . . . . .Pamela Salem

A big city journalist, writing a series on famous crimes, travels to Plampton, an East Anglian village to investigate its famous unsolved murder.

The Last Witness (2.6.71)

Directed by Michael Ferguson
Teleplay by Martin Worth

Cast:
Harris . . . . .Anthony Bate
Dr Benson .James Kerry
Mrs Kemble . . . . .Sheila Brennan
Sgt Waker .Lawrence James

Following being shipwrecked, Harris wakes up and finds himself recovering in a hotel on a small island. Periodically he gets flashes of what happened but has no clear memory. Finally it dawns on him that these glimpses are from the future and are building up to a dreadful and violent climax.

The Chopper (16.6.71)

Directed by Peter Cregeen
Teleplay by Nigel Kneale

Cast:
Chaser . . . . .George Sweeney
Jimmy Reed .Patrick Troughton
Sandie . . . . .Margaret Brady
Rupert Molloy . . . . .David Wood
Lorna Venn .Ann Morrish

Quatermass creator Nigel Kneale wrote this ghost story about the spirit of a dead biker haunting his wrecked motorbike, the 'chopper' of the title.

The Uninvited (23.6.71)

Directed by Eric Hills
Teleplay by Michael J. Bird

Cast:
George Pattison . . . . .John Nettleton
Millicent Pattison . . . . .June Ellis
Donald Ramsey . . . . .Brian Wilde
Jessica Ramsey . . . . .Hilary Mason
Jack Mervyn . . . . .Geoffrey Palmer
Frances Mervyn . . . . .Shirley Cain

A supernatural power haunts a middle-aged couple, creating waves of eerie disturbances during the hours of darkness.

The Shattered Eye (30.6.71)

Directed by Peter Hammond
Teleplay by David T. Chantler

Cast:
Lester . . . . .Freddie Jones
Alec . . . . .Richard Warwick
Gwenn . . . . .Tessa Wyatt
Gavin . . . . .Peter Arne
Barton . . . . .John Wentworth
Tony . . . . .Sebastian Breaks

A young painter's life is thrown into violent turmoil following a chance meeting with a sinister old tramp.

THE QUATERMASS EXPERIMENT

A TV phenomenon. The rather staid world of British television in the 1950s was given a real shaking with the trio of *Quatermass* serials that brought science fiction and horror to the small screen. Writer Nigel Kneale and producer/director Rudolph Cartier enjoyed a marvellous collaboration that not only resulted in the *Quatermass* stories, but also in the memorable 1954 adaptation of George Orwell's *1984*.

But before that was the first of the *Quatermass* stories, *The Quatermass Experiment* which introduced Professor Bernard Quatermass, the brilliant scientist who would be called upon many times to save the day for an entire planet.

BBC, 30 mins b/w
Created and Written by Nigel Kneale
Produced and Directed by Rudolph Cartier

The Quatermass Experiment: Isabel Dean and Reginald Tate on set

Cast:
Prof. Bernard Quatermass . . . . .Reginald Tate
Judith Carroon . . . . .Isabel Dean
Victor Carroon . . . . .Duncan Lamont
John Paterson . . . . .Hugh Kelly
James Fullalove . . . . .Paul Whitsun-Jones
Dr. Gordon Briscoe . . . . .John Glen
Chief Insp. Lomax . . . . .Ian Colin
Det. Sgt. Best . . . . .Frank Hawkins

Episode 1 ('Contact has Been Established') and Episode 2 ('Persons Reported Missing') both exist as 16mm telerecordings in the BBC archive. The following episodes are missing:

Episode 3: Very Special Knowledge (1.8.53)

Astronaut Victor Carroon is being taken back to the scene of his crash landing in Wimbledon; a recording of what happened is played back to him. This disturbs him greatly and his body starts to undergo a strange alien transformation.

Episode 4: Believed to be Suffering (8.8.53)

Fleeing from journalists Carroon takes refuge inside a cinema. His mutation continues; he goes to a chemist to try and get something for the pain.

Episode 5: An Unidentified Species (15.8.53)

Quatermass works out that the chemicals Carroon has taken will only accelerate his metamorphosis. They race against the clock to locate him before full mutation takes place but they seem to be too late when they learn of some killings and then witness a pulsating alien mass clinging to the side of Westminster Abbey.

Episode 6: State of Emergency (22.8.53)

A state of emergency is declared and the army are brought is to destroy the alien creature. This is to no avail however and Quatermass gambles on a last-minute plea to whatever remains of Carroon's humanity, buried deep within the alien organism.

All other *Quatermass* episodes survive. *The Quatermass Experiment* was remade for the big screen by Hammer Studios in 1955.

First Night: The Road

Nigel Kneale's name has been synonymous with TV fantasy since the early 1950s. His *Quatermass* series of sci-fi chillers and his memorable adaptation of George Orwell's *1984* are landmark television productions. In 1963 BBC Television produced what some critics would argue is Kneale's finest work, an atmospheric ghost story with a terrific pay-off. A major missing work of first-class, small screen fantasy.

The Road: John Phillips and James Maxwell

BBC (*First Night*) 29.9.63
55 mins b/w
Produced by John Elliot
Directed by Christopher Morahan

Cast:
Gideon Cobb . . . . .John Phillips
Sir Timothy Hassall . . . . .James Maxwell
Lavinia . . . . .Ann Bell
Big Jeff . . . . .David King
Lukey Chase . . . . .Victor Platt
Sam Towler .Rodney Bewes
Landlord . . . . .Reg Leaver

In 1770, scientist Sir Timothy Hassall clashes professionally with visionary philosopher Gideon Cobb as they investigate a supernatural phenomenon occurring in a wood supposedly haunted by an army slaughtered there during a bloody battle. But is this a genuine ghostly disturbance or is the effect caused by a ripple in the time continuum. Could it be that they are faced with a manifestation of the future rather than the past?

POP

Although the 1960s are revered as the golden age of British pop, an amazing number of pop shows from the period are missing from the archives. Take the BBC's flagship *Top of the Pops*, first broadcast in 1964, which featured all the chart hits of the day (and, in fact, continues to this day). There are only four editions of *Top of the Pops* surviving from the entire 1960s. These surviving editions are from: 26.12.67, 15.2.68, 6.6.68 and 27.2.69.

Other shows of the time have fared similarly badly (see following sections on *Thank Your Lucky Stars* and *Juke Box Jury*). The A-R series *Ready, Steady, Go!* has a much better survival rate, although accurate reports of what exists have been difficult to find.

THANK YOUR LUCKY STARS

Pitched partly as a response to the BBC's long-running *Juke Box Jury*, *Thank Your Lucky Stars* hit the ground running and grew from a 12-week experiment to a popular fixture in the ITV schedules. The format was simple – stars of the day (both British and American) would appear performing (miming) their latest release, introduced by Keith Fordyce and later Brian Matthew, a non-teenager who described himself as 'a sort of with-it uncle' (still later Jim Dale became the host). One segment of the show 'Spin A Disc' was uncomfortably reminiscent of *Juke Box Jury* with a panel voting on new releases. In 1962 Birmingham panel member, teenager Janice Nicholls, became a national favourite and was brought back as a regular, given ample opportunity to air her catchphrase 'I'll give it foive'. Hard to appreciate now but such regional accents were still a rarity on TV outside the kitchen sink drama – elsewhere BBC English still dominated the airwaves. This perhaps goes some way to explain the novelty of Ms Nicholls to an audience unused to hearing such 'real' people.

Thank Your Lucky Stars was popular with audiences and certainly attracted big name stars. The Beatles made their first national appearance on the show on 19.1.63 and were regular guests over the following couple of years. Only two broadcast-standard copies survive: the edition of 14.5.66 featuring The Rolling Stones and Tom Jones; and the last edition on 25.6.66 which featured The Beatles (on film), Herman's Hermits, Helen Shapiro and Gene Pitney. A 5-minute extract exists from the 10.2.62 edition (also featuring Gene Pitney) and there is a VHS recording of the 21.12.63 show (featuring The Beatles and other famed Liverpool acts).

All other editions of *Thank Your Lucky Stars* are missing, believed wiped. Any that have survived are likely to be 16mm telerecordings, although with the huge collector interest in such music acts there is always the possibility of VHS copies made from illegally held material.

Thank Your Lucky Stars
ABC 1.4.61–25.6.66 b/w

Editions of particular interest:

1.4.61 (Hughie Green, Anne Shelton, The Five Dallas Boys – 1st edition)

30.12.61 (Cliff Richard, The Shadows, Helen Shapiro, Billy Fury, Chubby Checker)

13.10.62 (John Leyton, Dion, Little Richard, Clinton Ford)

10.11.62 (Sam Cooke)

19.1.63 (The Beatles – first national TV appearance)

23.2.63 (The Beatles, Billy Fury, Jet Harris and Tony Meehan)

20.4.63 (The Beatles, Del Shannon, Johnny Tulotson, Bert Weedon, Mike Berry, Dave Clark Five)

18.5.63 (The Beatles, Petula Clark)

29.6.63 (The Beatles, Gerry and the Pacemakers, Billy J. Kramer, The Searchers)

13.7.63 (The Rolling Stones, Helen Shapiro)

24.8.63 (The Beatles)

14.9.63 (The Rolling Stones, The Searchers, Heinz, Brian Poole and the Tremolos)

26.10.63 (The Beatles, The Searchers)

23.11.63 (The Rolling Stones, Cliff Richard, The Shadows, Gene Pitney)

21.12.63 (see intro)

29.2.64 (The Rolling Stones, The Hollies, Big Dee Irwin, Kathy Kirby, Bobby Vee)

30.5.64 (The Rolling Stones, Adam Faith, Dionne Warwick)

20.6.64 (Jim Reeves, Alma Cogan, Dave Clark Five, P. J. Proby)

27.6.64 (Yardbirds, The Searchers, Elkie Brooks)

11.7.64 (The Beatles, Dusty Springfield, Manfred Mann)

8.8.64 (The Rolling Stones, The Merseybeats)

3.10.64 (The Rolling Stones, Heinz, Shirley Bassey)

21.11.64 (The Beatles, Alma Cogan, Freddie and the Dreamers [The Beatles segment survives])

5.12.64 (The Rolling Stones, Sandie Shaw, Petula Clark, Herman's Hermits)

27.2.65 (Roy Orbison, Dusty Springfield, The Zombies, Tom Jones, The Searchers)

27.3.65 (The Rolling Stones, Bobby Vee, Susan Maughan)

3.4.65 (The Beatles, The Animals, Dionne Warwick, The Drifters, Tom Jones)

12.6.65 (The Rolling Stones, The Kinks, Lulu)

4.9.65 (The Rolling Stones, Herman's Hermits, Unit 4+2, Lulu, Chubby Checker)

4.12.65 (The Beatles [on film], The Shadows, The Kinks, Tom Jones, Mark Wynter)

19.2.66 (Marc Bolan, Billy Fury, Lulu, The Animals, Peter and Gordon)

26.2.66 (Yardbirds, Tom Jones, Gene Pitney)

Colour Me Pop

One of the greatest losses of the time is *Colour Me Pop*, a late night BBC2 colour series which grew out of the contemporary arts programme *Late Night Line Up*. *Colour Me Pop* featured many of the 'more serious' performers of its day, usually devoting a whole edition to one artist. Some editions featured studio performances others went on location to present live concerts (from the Fairfield Hall in Croydon). Odd excerpts of the series have turned up in various places and there are rumours of shows existing in foreign archives which haven't been given back to the BBC. Here is a list of the missing complete programmes from the UK archives:

Produced and directed by Steve Turner
BBC, colour
14.6.68–30.8.68 (*Late Night Line-Up Presents Colour Me Pop*)
7.9.68–30.8.69 (*Colour Me Pop*)

14.6.68 (Manfred Mann)
28.6.68 (Eclection)
12.7.68 (Salena Jones with the Brian Lemon Trio)
19.7.68 (Fleetwood Mac)
26.7.68 (The Kinks)
9.8.68 (The Peddlers)
16.8.68 (The Tremeloes)
23.8.68 (Barry Noble)
30.8.68 (Spooky Tooth)
7.9.68 (The Hollies)
21.9.68 (Unit Four Plus Two)
28.9.68 (David Ackles)
5.10.68 (O'Hara's Playboys)
12.10.68 (Honeybus, Clodagh Rogers) – sections survive
2.11.68 (Eclection, Jethro Tull)
9.11.68 (Foggy Dew-O, Lew Prinz and the Bedrocks)
16.11.68 (The Nice)
23.11.68 (The Alan Price Set, Julie Driscoll, The Brian Augur Trinity)
30.11.68 (Giles, Giles and Fripp)
7.12.68 (Timebox)
14.12.68 (Love Sculpture)
21.12.68 (Bonzo Dog Doo-Dah Band) – sections survive
28.12.68 (The Hollies)
11.1.69 (Sons and Lovers)
18.1.69 (The Pop Tops)

25.1.69 (The Toast)
1.2.69 (Chicken Shack)
8.2.69 (Bobby Hanna and the Art Movement)
15.2.69 (The Equals, Barbara Ruskin)
22.2.69 (Marmalade)
1.3.69 (Ten Years After)
8.3.69 (World of Oz)
15.3.69 (Caravan)
22.3.69 (Harmony Grass)
12.4.69 (Free)
19.4.69 (Jimmy Campbell, Sweet Thursday)
26.4.69 (The Elastic Band)
10.5.69 (Family)
17.5.69 (Cats Eyes)
31.5.69 (Group Therapy)
7.6.69 (Lions of Justice)
14.6.69 (Strawbs)
5.7.69 (Trapeze)
12.7.69 (Copperfield)
26.7.69 (Orange Bicycle)
2.8.69 (The Love Affair, Philip Goodhand-Tait)
9.8.69 (Gene Pitney, Mike Cotton Sound)

DOCUMENTARY

Tyranny: The Years of Adolf Hitler

A flagship A-R documentary that looked back at the life of Adolf Hitler. Many other documentaries have covered this ground but few have the depth and ambition of this particular programme. Kenneth Harris of *The Observer* was our host telling the story of Hitler's rise and fall, posing certain questions to various interviewees: 'How could Hitler, who never even got a commission in World War I, have been allowed to overrule brilliant generals?' 'Could Britain have done more to stop Hitler's rise to power in the early 1930s?'

The programme went out live but there were filmed inserts for illustration purposes and of certain interviews shot in Germany. Hitler's chauffeur, Rudolf Kempke, was interviewed, as was

Tyranny: The Years of Adolf Hitler – director Peter Morley interviews Paula Wolf, Hitler's sister

Obersturmbannführer Julius Schaub. But most startling of all was the interview with Hitler's sister, Paula Wolf. It was an amazing coup which sparked newspaper headlines and earned rave reviews: 'As a TV programme *Tyranny* was the best documentary seen on the screen this year', said Ramsden Greig in the *Evening Standard*; '… as a TV documentary on Hitler – and there have been many – it was one step ahead of anything before', claimed James Thomas in the *Express*; '*Tyranny* gave a hint of the heights to which British television could rise if ITV went into hot competition with the BBC on subjects of social and political importance', gushed the *Leicester Mercury*.

It's unlikely that the programme has survived but sadly the filmed segments are also missing. Director Peter Morley lamented the loss in a newspaper article in the 1980s and soon afterwards was contacted by a Richard E. King who had audio recorded the programme when it went out and had kept the tape. He gave Morley a copy, so at least there is an audio record, but it would be a significant historical thing if the filmed inserts did re-emerge.

A-R tx 4.3.59, 50 mins b/w
Directed by Peter Morley
Written by Cyril Bennett
Presented by Kenneth Harris

THE US

Certain factors in the US ensured that many great programmes from the golden age survived. The different time zones meant that programmes would be kinescoped (telerecorded) for transmission a few hours later to certain territories. Also the policy of syndication (in which programmes once broadcast were sold on to local station affiliates) led to many copies being made of most shows. Finally, the nature of the major networks – which like Britain's Channel 4 acted more as a publishing house for independent productions – meant that individual companies made programmes for the major networks and naturally kept and looked after their output as it was a valuable resource in rerun and foreign sales.

Nevertheless some items have gone missing and there follows a list compiled by the US Museum of Television and Radio (MT&R), of TV material missing from the archives.

Lost US Programmes

Early Rod Serling dramas
1950–53

The MT&R is searching for programmes that *Twilight Zone* creator Rod Serling wrote early in his career, including numerous episodes of *The Storm*, a local Cincinnati series; Serling's first network teleplay, *Grady Everett for the People*, written for *Stars Over Hollywood*; and numerous episodes of *Lux Video Theatre*.

Actors Studio
1948–50

The MT&R are searching for any examples of this live anthology series produced by the legendary school for professional actors. Among the performers making very early television appearances are Kim Hunter, Julie Harris, Jessica Tandy, Martin Balsam and Marlon Brando.

Nightbeat
1955

Only one edition of Mike Wallace's influential interview series, an interview with *Playboy* founder Hugh Hefner, survives so far.

Open End
1958–66

Few episodes of David Susskind's early interview series remain. The Museum is particularly interested in the following Susskind discussions:

'The Young Giants' (1.2.1959) with directors Fred Coe, John Frankenheimer and Sidney Lumet;
'Always Leave Them Laughing' (14.2.1960) with comedy writers Larry Gelbart, Mel Tolkin and
      Mel Brooks;
'Television Tempest' (25.9.1960) with Ernie Kovacs, Rod Serling and Sheldon Leonard;
'Theater Below the Summit' (28.5.1961) with Joseph Papp, Fritz Weaver and Edward Albee;
and the 13.6.1965 debate between James Baldwin and William F. Buckley.

James Dean appearances on television
1951–5

James Dean appeared in more than thirty dramatic productions and the MT&R is searching for his work on the following series:

Big Story: 'Rex Newman' (1953)
Campbell TV Soundstage: 'Life Sentence' and 'Something for an Empty Briefcase' (1953)
Danger: 'No Room' and 'The Little Woman' (1953) and 'Padlocks' (1954)
Lux Video Theater: 'The Foggy, Foggy Dew' (1952) and 'The Life of Emile Zola' (1955)
The Kate Smith Hour: 'Hound of Heaven' (1953)
Philco Television Playhouse: 'Run Like a Thief' (1954)
The Web: 'Sleeping Dogs' (1952)
Treasury Men in Action: 'The Case of the Sawed Off Shotgun' and 'The Case of the
      Watchful Dog' (1953)
You Are There: 'The Capture of Jesse James' (1953)
G. E. Theater 'The Dark, Dark Hours' (1954) with Ronald Reagan

Early Gore Vidal Plays
1955–9

Gore Vidal began writing for television in the 1950s. The Museum is searching for the following live dramas for which he wrote the teleplay:

Philco Television Playhouse: 'The Death of Billy the Kid (1955)
Goodyear Television Playhouse: 'Visit to a Small Planet (1955)
Sunday Showcase: 'The Indestructible Mr. Gore' (1959)

The Tonight Show
1st October 1962

The Museum is looking for the premiere of Johnny Carson's hosting of *The Tonight Show*. The Museum has an audio recording of the programme, which featured Rudy Vallee, Tony Bennett and Joan Crawford.

Show Biz: An Entertainment History
1955

This NBC colour spectacular highlights fifty years of entertainment and features Buster Keaton recreating his original vaudeville routines. Also appearing are Groucho Marx, Rosemary Clooney and Eartha Kitt.

All in the Family
1968

Several pilots of Norman Lear's influential series were produced; the Museum is looking for the first one, entitled 'Meet the Justices'.

Rock 'n' Roll Show
4th and 11th May 1957

Alan Freed hosted the first network rock specials with special guests Sal Mineo, the Clovers, Screamin' Jay Hawkins and the Del-Vikings.

The I Love Lucy Movie

Mid-1950s Lucille Ball and her team produced a movie consisting of three television episodes and never-before-seen connecting material. The film was tested in California and then never released.

One Night Stand: The World of Lenny Bruce
1959

This documentary, produced by comedian Lenny Bruce, looks at the underbelly of New York City.

The Buster Keaton Show
1949–52

Legendary silent comedian Buster Keaton produced several short-lived series in Los Angeles, which were syndicated nationally.

Lost Sports Television Programmes

Baseball

World Series Games (1948–68) – Especially, Willie Mays's overhead catch in 1954, Don Larsen's perfect game for the 1956 Yankees and Pirate Bill Mazeroski's game-winning home run in 1960.
All Star Games (1948–68)
Roger Maris's sixty-first home run (1961)
One of Sandy Koufax's no-hitters
Bobby Thomson's pennant-winning home run for the New York Giants (1951)
Ted Williams's final game for the Red Sox (1960)
Roberto Clemente's final game for the Pittsburgh Pirates in which he gets his 3,000th hit (1972)

Football

Super Bowls I and II
1967/8
The Museum is searching for the first two Super Bowls, both won by the Green Bay Packers.
New York Giants vs Baltimore Colts Championship Game (1958)
NFL Championship Games 1959–66
First AFL Game
Ice Bowl Game, Dallas vs Green Bay (1967)

BASKETBALL

Wilt Chamberlain's 100-point game (1962)
Early NBA All-Star Games
Minneapolis Lakers Championship Games, 1949–50; 1952–4
Championship Games, Boston Celtics, 1957; 1959–66; 1968–9
Championship Games, Philadelphia 76ers, 1967

ICE HOCKEY

Championship Games, Detroit Red Wings, 1954–5
Championship Games, Montreal Canadiens, 1956-60; 1965–6; 1968–9
Championship Games, Toronto Maple Leafs, 1962–4
Championship Games, Boston Bruins, 1970, 1972
Early NHL All-Star games

Ron Simon
Curator – Television
The Museum of Television and Radio,
25 West 52nd Street,
New York, NY 10019,
Telephone: (00 1) 212 621-6680
Fax: (00 1) 212 621-6642
E-mail: Rsimon@mtr.org

AFTERWORD

The preceding information is just the tip of the iceberg, thousands of other items of equal importance are sadly missing, believed wiped. Every genre, indeed every sub-genre, has important gaps among the archive holdings.

Researcher Stephen Bourne, author of *Black in the British Frame: Black People in British Film and Television 1896–1996*, is a leading authority on the work of Black artists in British television. The missing items he would most dearly like to see rediscovered show how, even this relatively small field has been badly affected:

Three plays by Trinidadian dramatist Errol John: *Play Of The Week: Moon On A Rainbow Shawl* (ATV 5.1.60); *First Night: The Dawn* (BBC 17.11.63); *The Wednesday Play: The Exiles* (BBC 23.4.69)

Two plays by Jamaican writers: *Play For Today: In The Beautiful Caribbean* (BBC 3.2.72) by Barry Reckford; *Shakespeare Country* (BBC 17.5.73) by Alfred Fagon

Two musicals featuring American singer Elisabeth Welch: *I Gotta Shoe or Cindy-Ella* (BBC 1966) also featuring Cleo Laine and Cy Grant; *Take A Sapphire* (BBC 1966) with music and lyrics by Caryl Brahms and Ned Sherrin

Donald F McLean is concerned with the very early days of TV. Before the electron tube camera was developed in the mid 1930s, the only solution to television was a system that was mechanically scanned. Limitations in camera, electronics and broadcast frequencies meant that the television picture comprised only a few dozen lines and the video signal consequently could be handled as if it was audio, and even be recorded onto 78rpm discs.

In Britain in 1927-28, John Logie Baird experimented with recording his video signal onto shellac discs (Phonovision). Many years later, a few viewers captured the video transmissions from BBC Television programmes on Baird's 30-line TV system using domestic audio disc recorders. After computer restoration, these images have recently been restored to open a new chapter in the history of television broadcasting in Britain. The restored images can be viewed at http://www.dfm.dircon.co.uk .

To date, only Britain appears to have such a recorded heritage of its mechanical TV era. Given the plethora of mechanical systems at that time, in USA, Japan, Russia and Europe, it seems unlikely that Britain stands alone. Donald F McLean, author of *Restoring Baird's Image* (ISBN 0 85296 795 0), is interested in hearing from anyone who may have in their archives disc recordings of the video signal from early television.

Similar lists could be supplied by all of the researchers delving into the more esoteric areas of television. It's easy to lament the losses but we mustn't lose heart, as mentioned at the start of this journey this a treasure hunt and the reward for dogged digging, can be gems worth their weight in gold. Happy hunting.

REFERENCES AND ACKNOWLEDGMENTS

Kaleidoscope Research Guides

No serious researcher working in the field of television can afford to do without the wonderful *Kaleidoscope* books with their marvellous episode listings and survival status information. Guide creators Richard Down and Christopher Perry (and the rest of the Kaleidoscope team) have made a huge contribution to the world of television research. The regular Kaleidoscope events often feature screenings of recent rediscoveries and the organisers make every effort to encourage material holders to donate copies back to the official archives. Kaleidoscope is a non-profit making organisation with any financial gains going to their nominated charity the Royal National Lifeboat Institute.

Kaleidoscope Guides:
Drama
Comedy
Music and Variety
Children's Programmes
and other specialist publications are available from:

Kaleidoscope Publishing
47 Ashton Rd
Ashton
Bristol BS3 2EQ

Radio Times/TV Times

In the 1950s, 60s and 70s these listings magazines had quite extensive programme information including storyline details, comprehensive cast lists and accompanying articles (for the prestige broadcasts) which actually discussed the programme rather than profile the star. They are a vital record of the schedules of the day and often provide a mine of information on programmes now sadly missing.

The ITV/ITA Annual Guides

Beginning in 1963 these Independent Television Guides contain a wealth of information and (up to and including the 1972 edition) also feature extensive details on programme output. These contain far more useful programme information than the equivalent BBC Handbooks.

British Television

The BFI's major television book, lavishly illustrated, giving a complete overview of TV broadcasting in the UK. Written by Tise Vahimagi.

The Encyclopedia of TV Science Fiction
Roger Fulton's excellent Boxtree/TVTimes book (now in its fourth edition) offering extensive information and episode guides on fantastical television, both British and American, that has aired in the UK.

TV Detectives
Geoff Tibballs' Boxtree book impeccably covering the world of TV detectives.

The ITV Encyclopedia of Adventure
Dave Rogers' Boxtree/TV Times book offering in depth information on shows ranging from swashbucklers to spy thrillers.

Radio Times Guide to TV Comedy
Mark Lewisohn's indispensable guide to the world of TV comedy (BBC Books).

Play for Today: The Evolution of Television Drama
Irene Shubik's (recently republished) memoirs of a life spent in TV drama. (Manchester University Press)

Serials on British Television 1950-94
Ellen Baskin's tremendously useful guide to British serials.
(Scolar Press)

Dad's Army: The Lost Episodes
Jimmy Perry and David Croft's scripts for the missing episodes of the classic series (Virgin Publishing)

Contemporary spin-off merchandising
The novelisations and script publications that accompanied the original transmission of programmes also provide valuable information. Paperbacks of *The Likely Lads*, *A For Andromeda*, the *Doctor Who* series, and the scripts from *Till Death Us Do Part* and the *Quatermass* serials are typical of the kind of material which can prove useful in this field.

Primetime: The Television Magazine
Long defunct television appreciation magazine, the organ of the Wider Television Access group.

405 Alive Magazine
Essential reading for the really committed television nostalgist. Available from The Radiophile, Larkhill, Newport Rd, Woodseaves, Stafford ST20 0NP

Laugh Magazine

Thoughtful and well researched comedy magazine that often features articles on TV comedy. Available from PO Box 394, Caulfield East, Victoria 3145, Australia.

Timescreen

Another impeccably researched magazine that has on many occasions detailed the gaps in official archives and run accompanying articles.

The World Wide Web

Thousands of television and television related websites exist but remember these are created by enthusiastic fans and can inadvertently contain many errors. For every properly researched and factually accurate website there may be half a dozen flawed (though still entertaining and interesting) ones.

However for the dedicated enthusiast of the search for missing material there is one excellent site which combines information with a fascinating discussion forum where fans can share their finds, ask questions and receive, on the whole, precise and factual answers. This is Mark Brown's marvellous site which can be found at: www.missing-episodes.co.uk. Well worth a visit and is one sure way to keep up to date with events in this area long after this book is published.

ACKNOWLEDGMENTS

Special thanks to my friend and colleague Mark Lewisohn.

Some of the chapter information first appeared in articles in the Saturday *Daily Telegraph*'s Arts and Books section. Thanks to my editors there, Tim Rostron (now of Canada's *National Post*) and Caspar Llewellyn Smith.

Thanks are also due to Sue Malden (and the rest of the BBC's Treasure Hunt team), Christine Slattery, Steve Roberts, Ralph Montagu, Paul Vanezis, and the many private and professional collectors, archivists and enthusiasts that have aided and abetted with relevant information and/or the return of material.

My gratitude, also, to the television broadcasters (especially the BBC) who generously provided special permissions for use of photographic material.

INDEX